How to Catch a Cricket Match

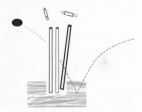

09

THE GINGER SERIES

how catch a
cricket match
harry ricketts

AWA PRESS

First edition published in 2006 by
Awa Press, 16 Walter Street,
Wellington, New Zealand

National Library of New Zealand Cataloguing-in-Publication Data
Ricketts, Harry.
How to catch a cricket match / by Harry Ricketts. 1st ed.
(The ginger series, 1176-8452 ; 09)
ISBN-13: 978-0-9582629-0-3
ISBN-10: 0-9582629-0-X
1. Cricket. I. Title. II. Series: Ginger series (Wellington, N.Z.)
796.358—dc 22j

Typesetting and diagrams by Jill Livestre, Archetype
Umpire signals by Scott Kennedy
Printed by Astra Print, Wellington
Printed on environmentally friendly and chlorine-free Lux paper.
This book is typeset in Walbaum

www.awapress.com

For my cricketing sons and stepsons
Max, Jamie, Tommy and Tom

ABOUT THE AUTHOR

HARRY RICKETTS was born in London in 1950 and grew up in England, Malaysia and Hong Kong. After reading English at Oxford University and obtaining a B Litt, he taught at Hong Kong and Leicester Universities, before moving to live in New Zealand in 1981. He is an associate professor in the School of English, Film, Theatre and Media Studies at Victoria University of Wellington. His poems, critical essays and literary reviews have appeared in journals in New Zealand, Australia, Hong Kong, France and the United Kingdom. Playing, watching and reading about cricket have been a central passion since childhood. In a long if never particularly illustrious career, he has played cricket in three continents, taken five hat tricks and scored two centuries.

ILLUSTRATIONS

CONTENTS

Cricket:
A sport
at which
contenders
drive a ball
with sticks
or bats in
opposition to
each other.

Samuel Johnson,
A Dictionary of the
English Language

Before the start of play

I T'S JUNE 1955. My father and I are playing cricket on our pocket handkerchief of a lawn. Our house is in a barracks just outside Worcester, and the lawn is surrounded by laurel bushes, with spikes on top of the walls behind. My father, an English army officer, is a quiet man with a salt-and-pepper moustache, rather shy. 'Good shot,' he says. 'Keep your eye on the ball. Hard lines.' When it's my turn to bowl, I run round and round the garden, whirling my arms and shouting, 'I'm Typhoon Tyson!' until I get giddy and fall over giggling.

August 1961. My father and I sit transfixed on blue-backed chairs in the study. On the black-and-white screen, England are 150 for 1 and need only another 100 more runs to win the Test against Australia and regain the Ashes. Ted Dexter is on 76, a thrilling innings. The Australian captain, Richie Benaud, is bowling round the wicket, pitching his leg-spinners in the rough outside the batsman's leg-stump.

Suddenly Dexter flashes at a ball and is caught by the wicket-keeper. A pity he's out, but no matter because in comes Peter May, the England captain and one of the best batsmen in the world. He looks relaxed, in control. Second ball, Benaud bowls him behind his legs for 0, playing a sweep shot without covering his wicket with the left pad – an elementary mistake.

The next batsman is Brian Close, a left-hander. Within minutes he too has committed cricketing suicide, sweeping. My father and I sit on in the blue-backed chairs, distraught, disbelieving, as almost-victory slides inexorably to defeat.

August 1976. The scorching English summer of Dutch elm disease. I am on holiday from my job in Hong Kong and staying with my friend David in Elvington, just outside York. David has secured us a game for the Elvington Second XI. The game – against the staff of a supermarket chain – takes place on the edge of a park. The pitch is an ordinary strip of mown grass, with the creases at each end marked out in white. It is a minefield, lethal. The ball either shoots along the ground or knocks your head off.

We make 48. David easily top-scores with 19. A shooter does for me, lbw 1. When their last man comes in, they are 48 for 9. One run to win, one wicket to tie. I've bowled throughout the innings, taken four wickets and sent another batsman to hospital – not intentionally: the ball simply reared up off a length and broke his glasses. The tension is palpable. What to bowl? Two short ones, I decide, followed by a yorker. The batsman leaves the first two balls, aims to swipe the third and win the game. The ball nips underneath the bat, hits leg-stump. The game is a tie.

January 1984, Wellington. From the garden comes the regular thud, thud of a tennis ball being thrown against a wall and hit back. My stepson Max is practising his batting. He's a left-hander, so he stands, side-on to the wall, bat in right hand, ball in left. I can picture the scene: his intense concentration as he throws the ball, then quickly grips the bat with both hands and lunges forward as the ball bounces back at him. He's not a natural sportsman, but by assiduous practice and great effort of will he has made himself a reasonable batsman. His knowledge of contemporary cricketers, both from New Zealand and overseas, is already encyclopaedic. How many did Martin Crowe score on his Test debut? (9 run out.) Who passed Freddie Trueman's record of 307 Test wickets? (The West Indian off-spinner Lance Gibbs.) It's a great bond between us. We often play down in Kelburn Park or on our scrap of lawn, just as my father played with me. Max also practises on his own for hours. Thud, thud.

It's now January 1990. My team — the one I've played for since 1982 — has a match at Tawa. We have only nine players. This is not good, nor is the fact we've scored only 80-something runs. I've brought my daughter Jessie (nine) and my second son Jamie (seven) with a picnic to watch the match. They both know how to play from Saturday 'Kiwi cricket' and games at home. We've batted hopelessly, but Tawa aren't strong and we still have a chance.

I ask the kids tentatively whether they'd like to field for us to make up numbers. They seem keen. I ask the Tawa captain if he minds. He doesn't. I tell the kids just to try and stop the ball if it comes near them, but on no account to try and catch it. I position Jessie at long-stop both ends, directly behind our wicket-keeper, a young journalist called John Campbell, and Jamie, who is more cricket-savvy, directly behind the bowler. Both make invaluable stops, and thanks to our left-arm spinner, Bede Corry, we win by half a dozen runs.

January 2001. My team (still the same one — at fifty, I'm now the oldest member) is playing a game at Granada North. Also in the team are Jamie, now eighteen, and another stepson, Tom. In itself it's not a particularly memorable game, but Jamie nonchalantly takes a high catch off Tom's bowling. The ball seems to hang in the air forever before coming down. Someone takes a photo of the three of us, in front of slopes of gorse, our eyes screwed up against the sun.

I sometimes ask myself what it is about cricket that has kept me playing and watching it with undiminished passion for half a century. And when I do, I blame my father. It was he who taught me the absolute basics of the game on that tiny lawn when I was five. 'Showed' is probably a better word. Cricket, as he showed it, went more or less like this. The person holding the bat was called the batsman, and stood in front of three sticks in the ground (the wicket) with two smaller sticks across the top (the bails). The person with the ball – usually my father – was called the bowler, and lobbed the ball at the wicket, trying to hit it. As the batsman, my job was to try to prevent the ball hitting the wicket, and, if possible, to whack it as far as I could.

It looked easy, but it wasn't. The ball, usually a tennis ball, would come towards me, fairly slowly. I would watch it all the way. It would bounce. I would swing the bat and often, somehow, miss. If the ball hit the wicket, my father would usually give me another go. He was infinitely patient.

That duel between bowler and batsman is the essence of cricket. The bowler is trying to hit the wicket. The batsman is trying to prevent this, and to hit the ball as far as possible. Everything else in cricket is merely an amplification of this essential encounter.

The first amplification is that in a real game of cricket – a match – there are eleven players on each side, plus two umpires. Each team takes it in turn to bat and bowl. The object is for one team to score more runs than the other. The object of the team that is fielding is to dismiss, or 'get out', ten of the batsmen on the opposing team.

All eleven of the bowling side are on the field at once, but only two batsmen; their team-mates sit on the sidelines.

In the middle of the field stand two wickets, 22 yards (20 metres) apart, with white-painted lines to show where the batsmen should stand – the 'batting crease' – and from behind which the bowler should bowl – 'the bowling crease'. One batsman faces the bowler; the other stands at the bowler's end, ready to run if required.

The section of the playing area to the right of the batsman who is facing the bowler is called the off-side; the section to the left (because it is the side where the batsman's legs are) is called the leg-side or on-side (see figure 1). Complementing this division of the cricket field into off-side and leg-side, the three stumps that comprise the wicket are referred to as the off-stump, middle-stump and leg-stump.

The second amplification is that there are ten ways in which the batsman can be got out. Five of these are common and happen in most matches. The most compre-hensive, and often dramatic, is when the batsman is

Figure 1 **The wicket**

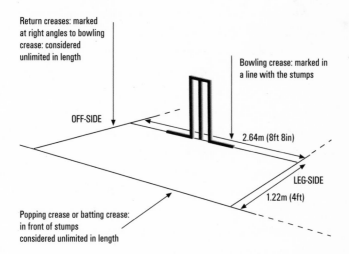

Return creases: marked at right angles to bowling crease: considered unlimited in length

Bowling crease: marked in a line with the stumps

OFF-SIDE

2.64m (8ft 8in)

LEG-SIDE

1.22m (4ft)

Popping crease or batting crease: in front of stumps considered unlimited in length

bowled: that is, the bowler delivers the ball, the batsman misses, and the ball breaks the wicket, causing one or both bails to fall off. Fast bowlers, in particular, love making the bails fly and the stumps leap out of the ground.

But the batsman can also be caught: the ball hits bat or glove and is then caught by a fielder before touching the ground. Or run out: while the batsman is attempting a run, a fielder throws the ball at the wicket to which the batsman's heading and breaks it, or a fielder with the ball in hand breaks the wicket. Or stumped: the fielder stationed close behind the wicket in gloves and pads – the wicket-keeper – takes the ball and breaks the wicket, the batsman having strayed out of the crease. Or lbw (leg before wicket): any part of the batsman or batsman's equipment is hit by the ball, which the umpire feels would have otherwise hit the wicket – although this form of dismissal is also a bit more complicated than this simple description would indicate, and the cause of frequent dismay and controversy (see figure 2).

The five less common ways of being dismissed really are uncommon. I've been out 'hit wicket' – that is, the batsman has broken his own wicket while playing a shot – but only once.

I've never been out, or played in a game in which anyone was out, for hitting the ball twice: that is, after hitting the ball, the batsman tries to hit it again for purposes other than defending their wicket.

Nor have I played in a match in which someone was out for obstructing the field: that is, the batsman deliberately prevented a fielder from, say, catching the ball. Nor for handled ball – when the batsman touched the ball with a hand not holding the bat – although two English batsmen, Len Hutton and Graham Gooch, have been given out in Test matches in this fashion.

Nor have I seen anyone being timed out – that is, when the incoming batsman deliberately took more than two minutes to get to the crease.

At school, my fellow cricketers and I would sometimes fantasise about these more bizarre ways of being out, and even willfully introduce them into our knock-up games.

Figure 2 **The lbw rule**

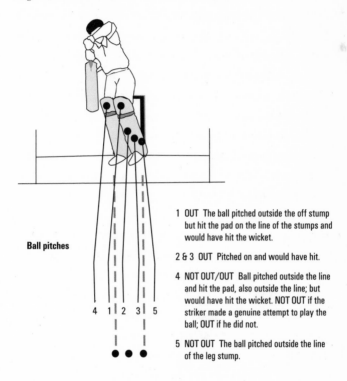

Ball pitches

4 1 2 3 5

1 OUT The ball pitched outside the off stump but hit the pad on the line of the stumps and would have hit the wicket.

2 & 3 OUT Pitched on and would have hit.

4 NOT OUT/OUT Ball pitched outside the line and hit the pad, also outside the line; but would have hit the wicket. NOT OUT if the striker made a genuine attempt to play the ball; OUT if he did not.

5 NOT OUT The ball pitched outside the line of the leg stump.

The third thing to grasp about cricket is that batsmen are not simply trying to stop themselves being out in any of these ten ways: they are also trying to score runs. A run is scored whenever a batsman facing a bowler hits the ball and the two batsmen successfully change ends without one of them being caught or run out. If they do this twice off the same ball, it counts as two runs and so on. If the batsman hits the ball on the ground across the boundary line, this is worth four runs and no actual running is required. A ball hit over the boundary line without touching the ground first is worth six runs.

Each run scored is accredited both to the team and to the batsman who scored it. But here's the confusing bit: the batsmen may also run if the ball ricochets off any part of the batsman's body (this is called a leg-bye), or is missed by the batsman but also by the wicket-keeper (a bye). Both leg-byes and byes are called extras, or sundries, and are accredited only to the team's score in the scorebook.

Cricket scorebooks or scorecards all follow the same basic format: the batsman's name, the mode of dismissal, the bowler's name, the batsman's total. Some even include a ball-by-ball breakdown of each batsman's innings – such as 'dot, 4, dot, bowled', or 'nothing scored, 4 scored, nothing scored, batsman out'.

Each batsman who bats has his or her own innings, or individual score: 4, say, or 60 not out. The team also has an innings, which is the combination of its batsmen's innings plus any extras. As an example, 250 all out means the team scored 250 runs and lost all ten of their available wickets; 250 for 7 means the team scored 250 runs but lost only seven of their ten wickets. Some matches involve one innings per side, some two.

Each bowler ordinarily delivers six balls to the same batsman – or to him and his partner, if they have changed ends due to an odd number of runs being scored. This is called an over. A right-handed bowler will normally bowl from the left side of the stumps and a left-handed bowler from the right. The ball must be delivered with a straight arm, or at least an elbow that does not bend more than 15 degrees. If the ball is not delivered with a straight(ish) arm, it is considered a throw, and the umpire calls 'no ball', giving the batsman, in effect, a free hit: the only way he can be out is if he is run out. He can't, for example, be out bowled or caught.

If the bowler's leading foot is in front of the foremost white line when the ball is released, the umpire also calls 'no ball', and an extra ball must be bowled. Some overs can, therefore, be ten or twelve balls long. Similarly, if a bowler bowls a ball beyond the batsman's normal reach, the umpire will call 'wide'.

For all dismissals except bowled and an obvious catch, the bowler and/or fielders must 'appeal' to the umpire. The appeal conventionally takes the form of 'howzat?' or, more plummily, 'how's that'.

Umpires use various fascinating signals to reinforce their decisions. If an umpire gives a batsman out, he raises his forefinger. If he has called a wide, he stretches out both arms to either side. For a no ball, he stretches out a single arm. A leg-bye is shown by tapping the leg, a bye by raising one arm above the head. A boundary four is indicated by sweeping one arm from side to side, a six by raising both hands above the head. Many umpires are known for their distinctive way of making these signals. When giving a batsman out, the New Zealand umpire Billy Bowden always raises a crooked finger, like a question mark.

At the end of each over, a bowler from the other end bowls to whichever batsman is now facing him.

If, in an over, a batsman fails to score any runs off the six balls, the over is called a maiden. Cricket is full of wonderfully strange names and terms like this: maiden over, gully, nightwatchman, yorker, googly and many others. (If in doubt, see the glossary on page 137.)

That's where poetry comes in. Fleming cuts Edwards to gully: as succinct as a haiku to a cricket follower; as impenetrable as the Enigma code to everyone else. Fleming cuts Edwards to gully: spelt out, it means the batsman, Fleming, plays a cut stroke to a ball delivered by the bowler, Edwards. A cut stroke is one in which a ball bouncing up outside the off-stump is hit with a horizontal bat to a fielder close in on the off-side, behind the batsman's wicket and between slip and point. But then you have to explain two other fielding positions, slip and point (see figure 3). A number of cricketing terms hark back to the eighteenth century, but gully is more recent, dating from only the early twentieth. It derives its name from the usual meaning of 'gully', implying the existence of a metaphorical channel between point and slip, towards the boundary behind the batsman.

Figure 3 **Fielding positions**

These are the most general fielding positions. They assume that the batsman is right-handed, and that the bowler is delivering right-arm over the wicket.

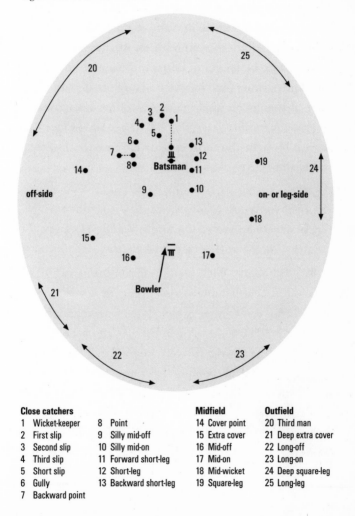

Close catchers		Midfield	Outfield
1 Wicket-keeper	8 Point	14 Cover point	20 Third man
2 First slip	9 Silly mid-off	15 Extra cover	21 Deep extra cover
3 Second slip	10 Silly mid-on	16 Mid-off	22 Long-off
4 Third slip	11 Forward short-leg	17 Mid-on	23 Long-on
5 Short slip	12 Short-leg	18 Mid-wicket	24 Deep square-leg
6 Gully	13 Backward short-leg	19 Square-leg	25 Long-leg
7 Backward point			

One of my favourite fielding positions is called silly mid-on. This refers to a fielder on the on- or leg-side of the pitch about 5 yards (4.5 metres) or so in front of the batsman. Mid-on – also a fielding position in its own right – is short for an older term, middle wicket on. The silly suggests the inherent silliness of standing so near the batsman, in danger of being hit when he strikes the ball. The position (and its name) date from at least 1878, when it was much used by an Australian team touring England. A century later, English singer-songwriter Roy Harper brought the term evocatively into the last song on his album *HQ*:

> *When an old cricketer leaves the crease*
> *Well you never know whether he's gone*
> *If sometimes you're catching a fleeting glimpse*
> *Of a twelfth man at silly mid-on.*

Twelfth man? Well, that's the substitute who can come on to field if someone is injured, or needs to leave the field for some other reason. A twelfth man isn't allowed to bat. Harper uses the term to suggest the ghostly presence of a retired player, lingering in that most absurd-sounding of fielding positions, silly mid-on. A yorker, incidentally, is a low full toss which passes under the batsman's bat, yorking him. This tricky maneouvre is rumoured to have been first used by Yorkshire players, hence the name. As for googly, a term probably first used in New Zealand, more of that later.

Where and how, then, did cricket, this most addictive and eccentric of sports, begin? Its origins are as uncertain as those of King Arthur and his Knights of the Round Table. Some think it is Celtic in origin. Some say it developed from medieval bat-and-ball games with names such as stool-ball, trap-ball and tip-cat. Some say Edward II played a version of the game as a boy in the fourteenth century. Some imagine the first players as two shepherds, one lobbing a stone at the other, who tries to hit it with his crook – and it is true that early cricket bats were curved at the end, rather like shepherd's crooks. There is a vast literature on the subject, and anyone interested will find the opening chapter of *Start of Play: Cricket and Culture in the Eighteenth Century* by David Underdown a handy starting-point. Two things seem certain: a game known as cricket was being played in Guildford, Surrey by the 1550s; and the birthplace of what eventually evolved into the modern game was in the Weald of England – that is, the 'forest counties' of Surrey, Kent and Sussex. It is documented that a team from the Weald played a team from the Downs in 1610 near Chevening in Kent.

One common misconception about cricket is that it started as a posh game. Not so, according to seventeenth century records, which report that in 1628 ten men from the Chichester area were fined a shilling apiece by the Archbishop's Peculiar Court for skipping church to play in a cricket match. The odd curate or esquire is referred to in the records, but there's no mention of dukes or earls. Some aristocrats probably played the game as boys, but as a class the aristocracy didn't get seriously involved until the 1700s, and then it took to the game with a will, as players, patrons, bettors and match-fixers.

The eighteenth century really put cricket on the map. The most enjoyable place to read about those early cricketing days and ways is John Nyren's *The Cricketers of My Time*. Published in 1833, this book marks the beginning of cricket literature – now by far the richest sports literature in the world. Nyren, who was born in 1764, reminisces about the men who performed for and against the Hambledon team of his Hampshire boyhood. He recalls how Noah Mann, an innkeeper, would ride 20 miles to practise on Tuesday evenings, and how the Revd Lord Frederick Beauclerk, a resourceful slow bowler, once lost his temper with Tom Walker, a farmer and obdurate opening batsman who lived up to his nickname, 'Old Everlasting':

> I remember Tom going in first, and Lord Frederick
> Beauclerk giving him the first four balls all on
> an excellent length. First four or last four made no
> difference to Tom – he was always the same cool,
> collected fellow. Every ball he dropped down just
> before his bat. Off went his lordship's white hat –
> dash upon the ground (his constant action when
> disappointed) – calling him at the same time

'a confounded old beast'. 'I don't care what ee
says,' said Tom, when one close by asked if he
had heard Lord Frederick call him 'an old beast'.
No, no, Tom was not the man to be flustered.

In addition to being an early stonewaller, Tom Walker is
famous for trying unsuccessfully to introduce overarm
bowling, which was not officially sanctioned until the
1860s. Before this all bowling was underarm.

It was the Victorian era which institutionalised
cricket, like so much else. The MCC – Marylebone
Cricket Club – was founded in 1787, but it was not until
the first half of the nineteenth century that the club
really took over the running of the game, and not until
1866 that it finally settled in London, at Lord's Cricket
Ground in St John's Wood, still considered the home
of cricket. From being a predominantly village game,
cricket was now widely played in towns, and an annual
county championship was set up. W. G. Grace, a huge
figure with a high squeaky voice and vast beard, and a
maestro with both bat and ball, became as famous in his
day as any of Lytton Strachey's Eminent Victorians,
Doctor Arnold, Cardinal Manning, Florence Nightingale
and General Gordon.

Ironically, at the very time cricket was being recognised as the quintessential English game, enshrined in
phrases such as 'It's not cricket' and 'Playing with a
straight bat', it was exported to the rapidly expanding

British Empire and ceased to be exclusively English at all. Most of the major British colonies soon became irrevocably hooked and have remained so ever since.

'Cricket is an Indian game accidentally discovered by the English,' begins Ashis Nandy's *The Tao of Cricket: On Games of Destiny and Destiny of Games*. His wittily subversive proposition speaks not just for India: you could equally claim cricket as a West Indian game. Indeed the book many consider the best ever written about the sport, *Beyond a Boundary* by the West Indian Marxist C. L. R. James, is a passionate paean both to cricket and to the emergence of West Indian identity. If you are Pakistani, Sri Lankan, Zimbabwean, Australian, Bangladeshi or South African, you could just as readily claim cricket as your national game.

Or if you are a New Zealander. On 28 December 1842, less than three years after the signing of the Treaty of Waitangi, the members of the Wellington Club organised a cricket match, Blues against Reds, on Te Aro flat. The Blues narrowly won, scoring 67 and 59 notches (runs) in their two innings and the Reds 64 and 60. This was followed by a slap-up Christmas dinner at Ship's Hotel.

March 1844 saw the first full match report of the 'truly English game of cricket' in the *Nelson Examiner*. Soon matches were being played all over the new colony, and areas were being set aside for general recreation, including cricket. In February 1864, Samuel Butler, sheep farmer and future novelist, wrote a piece of pseudo-Shakespearean blank verse describing how George Parr's visiting All-England Eleven comprehensively defeated twenty-two of Canterbury. The *Christchurch Press* printed it. The game had taken hold.

The way cricket was played in India, Australia, the West Indies and the other parts of the empire soon came to express something distinctive about those cultures. India produced wristy batsmen and wristy spinners. Australia produced bullish batsmen and bullish bowlers. The West Indies produced dashing batsmen and cyclonic fast bowlers. And New Zealand produced nuggety batsmen and economical medium-pace bowlers.

The more you know about cricket, the more you come to appreciate its drama, humanity and complexity. For some people, though, it never catches fire. One of these was Groucho Marx. Taken to watch a game, he asked, after it had been in progress for a while, when it was going to start.

Another is a friend of mine. 'Oh, I know all about cricket,' he says. 'You wear white clothes or pyjamas and first you're "in" and then you're "out". Like *Waiting for Godot*, it takes a long time, nothing happens, and there's usually rather a good tea.' More witheringly, Rudyard Kipling dubbed cricketers 'flannelled fools'.

For such refuseniks, there is no hope. For others, the best way to learn about cricket is to go to a game.

Just ones

and twos

on a pitch

Anne French, *with no lift.*
'Cricket'

Morning
session

I T IS SATURDAY, 18 March 2006, and I'm off to the Basin Reserve in Wellington to watch the second day of the second Test against the visiting West Indies. With me is Tony, an Aussie friend and colleague at Victoria University, who is writing a book about sport.

Tony and I became friends in classic cricketing fashion. Like all fans, the cricket fan is always on the look-out for fellow obsessives. A common tactic is to insinuate some cricket reference or piece of cricketing arcana into the conversation and see if you get a bite. The bait may be anything from 'And what about Murali's wrist?' to 'Strange that Jardine should be so keen on Hindu philosophy.' It's the cricketing equivalent of a pick-up line or Masonic handshake. This goes on all over the world and has done for centuries.

Alfred Hitchcock understood. In his 1938 thriller *The Lady Vanishes*, the comic relief is provided by a pair of cricket-mad upper-class twits, Caldicott (Naunton Wayne) and Charters (Basil Radford). While kidnappings, European espionage and romance unspool around them, all that bothers C and C is getting back to England in time for a Test match. Hitchcock understood the absurdity of the compulsion, but he also shared it. When the chips are down, he makes it clear, Caldicott and Charters are made of the right stuff and, twit or not, Caldicott knows which end of a revolver is which.

What exact piece of cricketing arcana Tony and I first exchanged I can't recall, but it was something to do with the great Australian leg-spinner Shane Warne – probably some back-of-the-hand allusion to his on-the-field heroics and off-the-field shenanigans.

Much of the pleasure of cricket lies in anticipation and speculation about what you are going to see, so as we start the 20-minute walk from Kelburn to the Basin, Tony and I are already previewing the prospects for the day's play. New Zealand – the Black Caps – won the one-day series easily enough, and the first Test match less easily.

The difference in the first Test, Tony asserts as we turn down Devon Street, was quite simply Shane Bond.

In both innings, the Black Caps' fast bowler dismissed Brian Lara, the premier West Indies batsman, with the first ball he bowled to him – for scores of 5 and 0 respectively. And when, with the Windies needing only 134 to win with 9 wickets standing, Bond forced Ramnaresh Sarwan to retire hurt, and then with the next ball bowled Lara behind his legs, the game tilted decisively in New Zealand's favour. This, we agree, taking a left into Aro Street, is one of cricket's great strengths as a game: within the larger contest between the two teams there is – ball by ball – the individual duel between a particular bowler and a particular batsman.

And, Tony goes on – his enthusiasm is infectious, also hard to stop once in full flood – it's not just that particular duel between bowler and batsman. It's what has come before and what the duel may lead to. Lara hasn't played in the one-day series: he has just come to New Zealand to play in the Test matches. At the time of the first Test he hasn't played much cricket for a while. Naturally he's a bit rusty. And he's in his thirties, so his reflexes aren't quite as quick as they were. He's not picking up the ball quite as early as he used to.

In the first innings, the ball from Bond is pitched short and rises on to him sooner than he expects, he is late on his pull shot (a shot played with a horizontal bat to a short, rising, straightish ball, literally pulling it to the leg-side), doesn't clear the fielder and is caught. So when he takes guard in the second innings, that dismissal is still on his mind. He is probably half-expecting another short, rising ball. After all, Bond has just hit Sarwan with such a delivery and forced him to retire hurt. So, literally and metaphorically, Lara is on the back foot. But the ball is pitched up on the line of Lara's body. He shuffles across his wicket to try and work the ball to leg for a single to get off the mark, misses – bowled.

And, Tony concludes, that duel between Bond and Lara – with everything that lay behind it – was the moment that decided the whole match. And all because Bond has the hoodoos on Lara. Hoodoos? I ask. As in 'voodoo', Tony replies. Bond brings him bad luck. Lara's now Bond's bunny, his for the taking.

Pity Bond isn't fit enough to play in this game, I say. Because that has been one of the talking points of the summer: can the injury-prone Bond, the Black Caps' only really fast bowler, stay fit enough to play the entire home season and then tour South Africa? But the answer to that is already no. Yet yesterday, the first day of this Test match, the Black Caps' second-string trio of quickish bowlers, James Franklin, Chris Martin and Kyle Mills, took eight West Indies wickets, including that of Lara, for under 200 runs. And who could have predicted that?

Now, already, we are at the Basin Reserve. I've lived in Wellington for 25 years and seen a good deal of Test cricket at the Basin, but it still gives me a kick as I push through the turnstile. The Basin is one of the prettiest cricket grounds I know. I'm particularly fond of the grassy bank which extends round the left-hand side as you enter from the city end. That, I like to think, is where the real punters go with their rugs and chilly bins and tinnies, although it's true that if you sit on the other side — in the partly covered R. A. Vance Stand, say — you have the added bonus of being able to look across at the bank and, rising above it, the backdrop of wooded Mount Victoria, where some of my favourite scenes in Peter Jackson's *The Lord Of The Rings* were shot.

The origins of the Basin Reserve are unusual. The place was originally a lagoon, joined to the harbour by a stream and known to the early settlers as simply the 'Basin'. There were plans to build a canal and use the Basin as a dock for ships. At the same time, the settlers were in search of a large flat space for their recreational pursuits. Then in January 1855 a serious earthquake raised the whole area five feet, turning the lagoon into a swamp. Plans for the canal were scrapped, and the swamp was drained, dug up and turfed. Within a few years the Basin Reserve was hosting rugby games, athletics meets, cycling races, military processions — and cricket matches.

Nowadays the Basin Reserve is, in effect, a huge traffic island. Sometimes a big hitter such as Chris Cairns will heave a ball out of the ground, and both play and traffic will stop while it's retrieved. The same thing used to happen when I lived in Hong Kong in the 1970s, although the 24-hour traffic which churned around the Chater Road ground was infinitely more relentless. I remember a friend, another Tony, hitting a massive six, and no one even thought of stopping play to look for the ball, lost as it was among the trams and taxis and rickshaws. That Tony was a police officer with literary aspirations, who went on to write historical blockbusters about the Far East.

Now, Aussie Tony and I aim for a section of the bank at the Adelaide Road end of the ground. You're almost behind the bowler's arm there, which provides a good view of the duel between bowler and batsman, particularly through binoculars. The only drawback is that you can't see the scoreboard very clearly.

It's an earlier start than usual to make up for lost time on the first day. Play is about to begin as we settle ourselves on the still slightly damp grass. There's a mackerel sky overhead and a bit of a wind, but it's warm enough for the spectators (a thousand perhaps already) not to have to be too bundled up. People around us slap on sunscreen, get sorted. As Stephen Fleming, the New Zealand captain, arranges the field for Franklin – plenty of fielders in the slip cordon, we notice – Tony and I again reflect on the overnight situation.

In a five-day Test match, the team that bats first ideally needs to score something like 400 runs (or at least 300) to feel they have the advantage. Cricket is about runs and wickets but also about time, so the aim is for the batting side to stay in for all or most of the first two days, making as large a total as possible before being bowled out or declaring. At this stage of the match (the beginning of day two), the fact the West Indies have compiled a score of only 182 and have lost 8 wickets in the process, including all their top batsmen, definitely puts them at a disadvantage. But, as someone always tediously points out: 'You never know with cricket.' Or, if they think they're a bit of a wag: 'It's a foony game, cricket' – delivered in an implausible Yorkshire accent.

However, today there are no surprises. The last two West Indies' wickets fall cheaply within a few overs to the steady Kyle Mills, who wouldn't even have been playing had Bond been fit. The players leave the field. West Indies: 192 all out.

Umpire signal: one short

A ghostly batsman plays to the bowling of a ghost.

Francis Thompson,
'At Lord's'

Break between innings

I'M MILDLY DISAPPOINTED at the smidgen of play we've watched so far. Rearguard actions from tail-end batsmen can be fun. Because they are in the side predominantly as bowlers, tail-enders are usually not very skilful as batsmen, but they often have a good eye and can hit the ball a long way. They are like the clowns, coming on to entertain the crowd in between the main events. In cricketing terms the clowning tends not to involve the batsmen falling over their own feet, although this has been known, but more a mixture of outrageous slogs, airshots and snicks, which can produce useful runs as well as high catches (sometimes dropped), not to mention farcical near misses and run-outs.

Today there have been no big hits, no action, just rather tame capitulation. Also, I'd hoped that Chris Martin might pick up the two remaining wickets. Martin got two wickets yesterday, but this morning the only bowlers have been Franklin and Mills. Tall, thin, shaven-headed Martin is a bowler, pure and simple. He's not a particularly good fielder, and he's a number eleven batsman who would go in even lower in the batting order if there were any lower to go. I've always warmed to cricketers like him who don't seem naturally sporty at all, but have this one rather odd aptitude of being able to bowl highly effectively.

Sometimes this aptitude depends on an accident of nature. In the 1970s India had the bewildering spinner B. S. Chandrasekhar, whose leg-breaks got extra whip from his polio-stricken bowling arm. Now Sri Lanka have Muttiah Muralitharan, the off-spinner with the weirdly bent elbow and revolving wrist. The Australian 'mystery' spinners Jack Iverson and J.W. Gleeson, both of whom flicked the ball off a folded middle finger, also come into this category.

Part of Martin's appeal for me is that he has a rather prancing run-up as he comes in to bowl and this reminds me of a medium-fast bowler called Bob Carter, whom I used to watch as a teenager in England at the Worcestershire county ground – another pretty ground, just by the River Severn with the cathedral in the background. Carter's nickname was the Galloping Major because of the rather clumsy way he used to run in to bowl, which was like nothing so much as a hefty horse.

The other thing about Chris Martin is that he has a streak of poetry about him. In interviews he doesn't trot out stock cricketing clichés of the 'Well, Smithy, I just tried to put the ball on the spot and let the pitch do the work' variety. Talking to Wellington sports journalist (and former fast bowler) Jonathan Millmow, for instance, he described how, if you take too much notice of what's said about you in the media, 'it's quite easy to get a little bit of static in the old head.'

'A little bit of static in the old head': John Snow, another of my fast-bowling heroes from the 1960s and '70s, would have understood that. Snow was solitary, moody but, when in the mood, capable of taking wickets at any moment. He was also capable of flat spells, when he seemed bored and merely going through the motions. Snow could be difficult. He once barged the diminutive Indian opener Sunil Gavaskar in a Test and was dropped for the next match. But this natural volatility, this unpredictability, was part of what made Snow appealing to me. That and the fact he wrote poems. One of Snow's best pieces, 'Lord's Test', catches something all bowlers have felt: 'On you toil again/across the width of the afternoon'. Another describes the sensation of being dropped from the side and feeling 'you have no middle'.

Martin, as far as I know, doesn't write poems, but you feel he could.

That's what happens when you watch cricket: one player or incident always reminds you of another. The game you're watching is constantly ghosted by memories of other games you've watched or played in or read about. Chris Martin's run-up makes me think of Bob Carter. His streak of poetry recalls John Snow. And from John Snow it's a short step to an earlier fast-bowling hero, Freddie Trueman. When I was eleven, I spent hours pretending to be Trueman. Like other fast bowlers of the time, the Yorkshireman wore a metal cap on the toe end of his right boot because of the way he dragged his back foot in his delivery stride. I wrecked several pairs of sandals imitating that raking drag on the prep school playground. Prep school, summer 1961: that's where my really serious addiction to cricket began. Other names, even more potent than Carter, Snow and Trueman, press in: Tom Graveney and Johnny Ussher. But New Zealand are about to start their first innings, and Tony is keen to mull over the prospects of the Black Caps' opening batsmen.

Umpire signal: call for television umpire

That which never really seamed

against that which was never really willow.

James Brown,
'The Crickets'

New Zealand's first innings

SOMETHING CRICKET watchers are keenly aware of, certainly at Test match level, is the relative significance of a particular game for particular players, and how they are likely to approach it. For instance, when a batsman with a secure place in the side comes in to bat, the watcher knows more or less what to expect: this batsman is naturally attacking, and likes to hit an early four to assert authority over the bowler; that batsman is more defensive, and initially likes to leave as many balls as possible and slowly accumulate runs. Similarly, some bowlers like to bowl a maiden over first, while others attack from the word go, not worrying about giving away runs. The expectations are different again with a player making their debut, or one still trying to establish a place in the team.

That is more or less the case with both of New Zealand's opening batsmen in this match, Hamish Marshall and Jamie How. Marshall has been playing Test cricket for a couple of years now with some success but, as Tony and I agree, he is not a natural opener. He made his mark as a steady middle-order batsman with a sound technique, who was good at working the ball into gaps in the field. (This ability to work the ball, and Marshall's curly hair, remind me of my son Jamie as a small boy. He knew he wasn't strong enough to hit the ball far, so he would push it and run.)

Nonetheless, the New Zealand coach, John Bracewell, has been trying to turn Marshall into an opening batsman. The wisdom of this has been fiercely debated in the media and among the cricket-following public, most of whom, like us, consider Bracewell hopelessly wrong. Marshall failed to make runs in both innings in the first Test at Eden Park; today could be an absolutely decisive moment for him.

Jamie How's situation is somewhat different. He is a regular opening bat and an attacking one, but he didn't do much in the first Test and is still very much a newcomer at Test level.

For both or either of these batsmen to succeed here could mean a great deal.

Within minutes Marshall is out, and the Black Caps are three runs for one wicket. Marshall had tried to push a ball from Ian Bradshaw (left-arm, medium-pace) through the leg-side and, getting a leading edge, dollied an easy catch to the West Indies captain, Shivnarine Chanderpaul, at short extra cover on the off-side. Tony and I nod wisely; this is as we had expected. In itself, the dismissal may have been a bit lucky, but it was a good tactical decision of Chanderpaul's to have a fielder in that precise position. He was probably hoping that the new ball, with its more pronounced seam, might 'stop' a bit on pitching, and that a checked or mistimed off-drive would provide a catch to a fielder there. That wasn't quite how it worked out, but he got the wicket anyway.

Chanderpaul has started with a conventional enough field setting for his quicker bowlers: plenty of slips and catchers close to the batsmen, only a long-leg out on the boundary. This is sometimes called 'crowding the bat'. The expectation is that, because the new ball usually swings in the air, batsmen are likely to misjudge the line and snick catches to the slips, wicket-keeper or other close catchers. In addition, the presence of most of the fielding side crouched around tends to be a bit intimidating for the batter and can help produce a false shot.

Captains often employ particular field settings for a particular batsman, knowing that, early on in his innings, he is prone to play the cut, say, or the hook shot. The idea is that before he has his eye in the batsman may not properly control the shot, and may hit the ball in the air and be caught. For such batsmen, fielders will be placed in particular positions (two gullies, perhaps, for someone with a marked penchant for the cut), and the bowler will try to land the ball on the right spot to encourage the shot. The batsman is, of course, aware of this, but it's surprising how often a plan like this works.

Once a batsman gets established, the captain will usually move the fielders back into more defensive positions in an attempt to stop him scoring, hence (perhaps) frustrating him into playing a rash stroke. The principle is the same with a spin bowler, although the exact field placings will vary because of the ball's relative lack of speed.

That was the last ball of Bradshaw's over. Fidel Edwards starts a new over to How. At the beginning of making his stroke, How tends to pick his bat up at an angle towards third man, rather than straight. He does so now, is late on his shot, and manages only an inside edge. A fraction of an instant later, his middle- and leg-stumps leap out of the ground. Edwards runs down the wicket, beaming. As he does so, he waggles the fingers of his left hand in front of his face in a gesture which over the summer has become familiar to spectators in New Zealand. No one (except his team-mates presumably) seems to know what the gesture means but it's certainly memorable, and there will already be kids copying it in playgrounds around the country.

New Zealand are now three runs for two wickets. This is serious.

As How walks disconsolately back to the pavilion, Tony and I assess Edwards as a fast bowler. Although on the short side, he is quick, with a stiff-legged approach to the wicket. The speedometer clocks some of his deliveries at well over 144 kilometres per hour (90 miles per hour). That's faster than Bond, although not, Tony points out proudly, as fast as the Australian Brett Lee, who has been logged in the 150s – as Bond also was, before a back injury cut the sharpest edge off his pace. Probably the fastest bowler ever is the Pakistani Shoaib Akhtar, whose bowling has reached 160 kilometres per hour (100 miles per hour). Thinking of West Indian fast bowlers, says Tony casually out of the blue, give me the title of Wes Hall's autobiography.

Wes Hall was a 1960s West Indian fast bowler who took an immensely long run-up to the wicket. He used to wear a gold crucifix around his neck, and as he bounded in, arms whirling, the crucifix would shake free, bounce off his chest and flash in the sun. He must have presented a terrifying sight to the batsman. In fact I know he did, because John Martin, a master at my public school, told me so. Martin had opened the bowling for Oxford in 1963 when the West Indies were touring England. Back then, a fast bowlers' union operated, whereby one fast bowler didn't deliberately aim to hit another. All the same, accidents did happen, and Hall was then acknowledged to be the fastest bowler in the world. John Martin was frankly terrified when he went in to bat at number eleven.

Initially he had a few balls still to face from a reassuringly slow bowler, but Hall was bowling at the other end. As Martin approached the wicket, he decided that facing Hall was the very last thing he wanted to do. The first ball from the slow bowler was a nice friendly full toss. With considerable relief, John Martin patted the ball gently towards mid-off and set off at once for the non-existent single run. He was comfortably run out at the bowler's end – just as he had hoped – and didn't have to face Hall.

I tell Tony the story. He laughs. It's a good story and could well be true. The appropriate edition of *Wisden*, the cricketer's bible which appears annually, lists J.D. Martin as run out 0 in the second innings of that match, and slow off-spinner Lance Gibbs as the bowler of the uncompleted over. Telling the story also gives me time to dredge up the title of Wes Hall's autobiography. *Pace like Fire*, I say, as though I'd known it all along.

So Edwards, although not of absolutely express pace, is pretty nippy. But what's tricky about his bowling is not so much his speed as his slingy action: he delivers the ball almost round-arm from behind his back, rather like the Australian fast bowler of the 1970s Jeff Thomson. This means that the batsman picks up the line of the delivery somewhat later than they normally would. The Sri

Lankan fast bowler Lasith Malinga bowls in a similar fashion, although he is even more round-arm, so much so that when he releases the ball it often seems to emerge from the umpire's stomach – very unnerving for the batsman.

The ball with which Edwards cleaned out How was not, it turns out, very fast at all – only 125 kilometres per hour. More of a 'sighter'.

The crowd, which has been steadily growing, is now tense, expectant. Peter Fulton, who came in at number three to replace Marshall, is playing in only his second Test match and hasn't yet faced a ball. He is joined by Stephen Fleming, who, with Nathan Astle, is one of the team's two most consistent batsmen. Edwards has five balls left in this over. If Fleming goes early, the West Indies will definitely have broken through.

It's one of those mini-duels between bowler and batsman (like Bond against Lara) which could turn the game, the individual confrontation within the larger drama. Fleming never got going in the first Test, but he did bat impressively in the earlier one-day matches, once hitting three consecutive balls for six over deep point. He is an elegant batsman, as left-handers often are, and rarely seems hurried in playing his shots. He 'has time', as cricket aficionados like to say. Didn't Edwards scone Fleming in one of the one-dayers? asks Tony hopefully. Yes, I say, and Astle. Not to mention Styris in the second innings of the first Test.

Being hit on the head — 'sconed' — is one of the occupational hazards in cricket. Before batsmen took to wearing helmets as a matter of course in the early to mid 1980s, you sometimes feared for their lives. An instance was the third morning of the first Test between New Zealand and Australia at the Basin in March 1982, which produced one of the tensest twenty minutes of cricket-watching I've ever experienced. John Morrison, later to become a laconic cricket commentator, was batting. The bowler was Jeff Thomson of the javelin-like action. The light was poor, the atmosphere overcast. Thomson was the fastest thing I've ever seen. Morrison clearly couldn't pick him up at all; you expected him to be badly hit at any moment, just wanted him to get out. When Rodney Marsh dropped him, there was no sense of elation. It simply prolonged the agony. Finally Thomson bowled Morrison, breaking two stumps. The relief. Edwards isn't as quick as Thomson but, like him, he can bowl a very hard-to-spot bouncer.

In addition to the Edwards–Fleming duel, this is one of those moments when the role of the bowling side's captain can be crucial. Both openers are gone. If Fleming, too, can be removed quickly, 192 won't look so bad a score after all. Chanderpaul already has an attacking field with three slips and two gullies. Should he now bring up a close catcher on the leg-side — move short mid-wicket up 20 yards to short-leg, say — to create extra pressure on Fleming? A more attacking captain probably would.

Tony and I briefly reflect on cricket captains famous for their ability to exert psychological pressure on opposing teams. The obvious example, grudgingly conceded by Tony, is Mike Brearley, captain of England in the late 1970s and early '80s. In the 1981 Test series against Australia, Brearley's ability to defend low totals by astute field placings and inspired bowling changes was as integral in turning a 1–0 deficit into a 3–1 winning margin as the all-round heroics of Ian Botham.

Geoff Howarth, the New Zealand captain of the same period, was equally adept at pressurising batsmen. An over or two before a break in play, he would often bring on a slow bowler like Stephen Boock and surround the batsman with a cordon of close fielders. Batsmen, desperate not to get out at such a key moment, would often lose their wickets by becoming overcautious or, conversely, overaggressive.

It takes confidence, of course. Despite his trademark silver-black blaze of war-paint on each cheekbone, Chanderpaul is not confident and has a poor record as captain. This is not entirely his fault: the current West Indies team is a shadow of the famous sides of the 1960s and '80s. Consequently, Chanderpaul's hold on the captaincy is shaky and he's reluctant to take risks. He leaves the field as it is. The plan is plainly to bowl at Fleming's off-stump and hope Fleming will nick a catch to the wicket-keeper or the slips, or for a short-pitched ball to jump from the shoulder of his bat to one of the gullies. It's a reasonable plan, but not an adventurous one.

The other part of the equation is Fleming's attitude. Faced with this crisis, will the New Zealand captain be ultra-defensive? Or will he respond more assertively, and by playing shots try to wrest the initiative back from the West Indies? Edwards has five more balls to bowl to complete his over. Fleming negotiates them calmly enough. In fact, Edwards lets Chanderpaul down by failing to bowl sufficiently straight. Fleming is able to watch several balls pass harmlessly outside his off-stump without having to offer a shot. This is bad bowling. By the end of the over, Fleming already looks settled. Fulton, too, seems composed. He opens his scoring off his first ball, driving Bradshaw for four, but otherwise he just defends while Fleming gradually takes charge.

In the first Test, Bradshaw dismissed Fleming in both innings – a significant moral advantage to take into this encounter. But in that match the ball was swinging a bit in the air and moving off the pitch. Here, both atmospheric conditions and pitch seem relatively unre- sponsive. Bradshaw bowls, a bit short on the off-side. Fleming moves onto the front foot, leans back a fraction and wristily chops the ball to the cover boundary. Four runs. A shot of authority. Over the next few overs he plays a string of similar shots off Bradshaw, each time for four.

The pressure starts to ease, and eases further when Edwards is replaced at the R. A. Vance Stand end by

Daren Powell. Powell looks like a typical West Indian fast bowler, tall with a raw-boned action, bit open-chested, mostly slanting the ball into the right-handed batsman. His pace is just under 140 kilometres per hour. Fulton doesn't look entirely comfortable against him but Powell doesn't make him play often enough, bowling a line a bit too wide of the off-stump.

Then during the twelfth over — Bradshaw's sixth — Fleming suddenly cuts loose. He chops a four through the seven-man off-side field, then swings a six effortlessly over mid-wicket, and punches two on-drives for four apiece. The New Zealand score jumps from 30 to 48 for 2: Fleming now has 39. Fulton is still on 4. New Zealand have been batting for only an hour. The umpires call for drinks.

Umpire signal: boundary six

That sweet

disorder

of the

youthful mind,

R.C. Robertson-Glasgow,
Crusoe on Cricket *cricketomania.*

Drinks break

TOM GRAVENEY and Johnny Ussher. These two were my special cricketing heroes when I was eleven. I first saw Graveney bat at the Worcester county ground in April 1961. Before that he had been just a name to me, although I knew my father thought him a great player. Now he had shifted to Worcestershire after a row with his old county, Gloucestershire, and this game against Richie Benaud's touring Australians marked his debut for his new county. Up to this point my serious cricket-watching had been limited, and this match against the mighty Australians was the first significant grown-up game of cricket I'd ever been taken to see. We were going for the full day, 11 am to 6 pm; we had a picnic and everything.

According to *Wisden* there was a biting wind, the wicket was soft and slow, and Australia were dismissed for a modest 177. I don't remember that. What I remember is Graveney coming in to bat late in the day with Worcestershire already deep in trouble. Keenly aware of my father's view of Graveney, I couldn't understand why at first he kept playing and missing the ball. When I anxiously pointed this out, my father explained that Graveney was missing the ball on purpose: he was simply playing himself in, gauging the pace of the pitch. At the time I was totally convinced by this explanation, and it's true that Graveney was soon persuading the ball through the off-side in his inimitable fashion. Years later I wrote a poem about the occasion and how, according to my father, Graveney had deliberately played and missed. I dedicated it to my son Jamie. When I showed it to him, he was sceptical, suggesting grandpa had probably been trying to allay my evident anxiety. This is possible, although I still like the idea of a batsman testing out the pitch in that way. In any event, that was the moment I got hooked on Graveney, and until he retired a decade later his score was always the first I looked for in the newspaper.

A month after first seeing Graveney, I was batting with my other hero, Ussher, an older boy at my prep school, Yardley Court in Tonbridge, Kent. It was my first match for the First XI. I was in the team as a bowler, not a batsman, and we were 62 for 9, chasing 83, when I went in as last man. Ussher (or Johnny, as I'd never have been cheeky enough to call him) had fair hair and ears that stuck out. He was the best bat in the side, better even than the captain Bob Woolmer, nicknamed 'The Unbowlable'. If this had been the kind of schoolboy cricket story (such as Siegfried Sassoon's 'The Flower Show Match') that I already liked reading, Ussher and I would have won the game, and I would almost certainly have made the winning hit. In fact, after a bit of a stand, Ussher was bowled for 40 trying to protect me from Ellerker, the other team's fast bowler, and we lost by eight runs.

Ussher left at the end of that term, but over the next few years I followed his cricketing fortunes. He went to the neighbouring public school, Tonbridge, and in July 1965 scored 60 not out in their annual fixture against Clifton at Lord's. Later he went on to become a doctor. It was Woolmer who became the cricketer, scoring three Test 100s against Australia in the 1970s and turning into a successful county and international coach. Woolmer, I remember, wasn't very popular at school and was generally considered rather thick. He was a good captain, though, and kind to me, the youngest member of the team. In his 1984 autobiography *Pirate and Rebel?* he reproduced a photo of that 1961 prep-school XI. He is sitting in the centre, a smirk on his face, and Ussher is to his right, ears sticking out. I am standing in the back row, directly behind my hero.

I can bowl so slow that if I don't like a ball I can run after it and bring it back.

J. M. Barrie,
on himself as a bowler

Morning session, continued

AFTER DRINKS break, Edwards comes on to bowl for Bradshaw. In the first Test Bradshaw had both taken wickets and kept the runs down. Now Fleming has hit him out of the attack, and forced Chanderpaul to bring back his main strike bowler – a reward for Fleming's bold stroke play. Edwards does indeed stanch the runs, and bowling round the wicket at Fleming sets a few problems, particularly with his well-concealed slower ball. Fulton at last comes out of his shell and cuts the persevering Powell for four. Powell retaliates by going wide on the crease and hitting Fulton on the shoulder with a sharply rising delivery. The next ball is pitched up, an intended yorker; intelligent bowling, this. But Fulton sees it early and drives handsomely for another four.

During Edwards' short spell, Fleming plays within himself, seemingly content to stop the straight ones and leave everything else alone. Then he leans on a wide one and takes four behind square on the off-side. Fleming 47. With a short mid-wicket and short extra cover in place, the plan still seems to be to get Fleming caught, lofting a mistimed drive. However, the chance is created in a different way altogether. Edwards bowls a short rising ball along the line of the body. Fleming swivels, hooking compulsively, and is late on the shot. He gets a top edge which steeples up high towards Powell, down on the boundary at long-leg. It doesn't look a particularly difficult catch, but perhaps Powell doesn't pick up the ball against the background. At any event he overruns the ball and fails even to lay a hand on it. Edwards puts his hands behind his head, distraught. Fleming and Fulton canter through for an easy two.

That would – should – have made the score 73 for 3. The crowd, which has held its collective breath while the ball was up in the air, lets it out. Tony, shaking his head in bewilderment at the missed catch, points out that such moments determine matches. With Fleming out, Edwards fired up by taking a wicket, and with still half an hour left until lunch, the West Indies might well have dismissed another batsman, even two. Suddenly the complexion of the game looks entirely different. 'Catches win matches,' as Woolmer used to say, and of course it's true. Yesterday the New Zealanders held their catches, which is why the Windies' total is so small.

Chris Gayle comes on to bowl for Edwards. Gayle, also an exciting opening bat, bowls off-breaks, and took useful wickets in the first Test. Gayle is Mr Cool. Tall and languid, he keeps sunglasses on even while bowling, and lounges up to the wicket as casually as if he's ordering a cocktail at some Caribbean bar. He usually bowls at around 90 kilometres per hour. He doesn't spin the ball in from the off much, just makes it drift away from the batsman in the air and dip a little in flight.

Fleming takes a leisurely single off Gayle and goes to his 50 at a run a ball. Although an expected rate in a one-day game, this is fast for a Test match. It's Fleming's 41st score between 50 and 100 in 168 innings in 98 Tests. He has also scored eight 100s.

For a batsman of his obvious class, Fleming's conversion rate from 50s to 100s is poor, as Tony enjoys mentioning. Fleming's total aggregate in Tests is 6147 runs at an average of 39.15. By contrast, Ricky Ponting, the current Australian captain, has scored 34 fifties and 31 centuries in 175 innings in 105 Tests, for a total of 8792 runs at an average of 58.23. (A batsman's average is calculated by dividing the number of runs he has scored by the number of times he has been dismissed; a bowler's by dividing the number of runs scored off him by the number of wickets he has taken.)

Tony lets Fleming's and Ponting's respective figures hang in the air between us. And then there's Bradman, he says conclusively. Sir Donald Bradman ('The Don'), as he doesn't need to add, scored 29 hundreds in 80 innings in 52 Tests. Total: 6996 runs at an average of 99.94. In other words, Bradman scored a century at better than every three Test innings he played.

I know, I concede, but he was the greatest batsman there's ever been. All the same, says Tony a little smugly, you know a serious Test average starts at 40.

Cricket fans love to mull over such statistics. For the cricket-averse, this is among our more annoying habits. Who cares, they say, that Sydney Barnes took 189 wickets for England in only 27 Tests? Or that at one time the New Zealand fast bowler Danny Morrison held the record for the most Test ducks? Or that Martin Crowe needed only one more run against Sri Lanka here at the Basin Reserve to become the first New Zealander to score 300 in a Test innings? Or that Bradman would have ended up with a Test average of exactly 100, had he scored just four runs in his last Test innings at the Oval in 1948?

Cricket fanatics care desperately about such things. Cricket is particularly statistics-friendly, and we find deep satisfaction in being able to recall abstruse facts and figures. No one would pretend, though, that a cricketer's stats were the final word on that particular player's quality, ability or value to their team. In fact, for the serious fan (although obviously not for the man himself) there is probably an extra satisfaction that Martin Crowe's highest Test score will remain forever 299 and not 300, and that Bradman, in his final Test innings, was bowled second ball by an Eric Hollies googly for 0, and consequently his Test average will remain frozen on 99.94.

99.94: this element of slight imperfection, almost-but-not-quite completion, is, Tony and I agree, cricket's reminder of human fallibility and the vanity of human wishes. We are jerked back from such philosophising by an even more blatant example. Fulton, with the lunch break only a few balls away, suddenly launches into an expansive drive at Gayle and, beaten in the flight, merely lifts the ball to Edwards at mid-off. It is an absolute 'sitter'. But, unaccountably, Edwards not only fails to catch the ball but allows it to hit his chest and bounce away behind him for four. Perhaps his mind was already on lunch. That would have been 81 for 3, and Fulton out for 23. It's the second lucky let-off in 20 minutes.

The leg-spinner Rawl Lewis is given the final over before lunch. Some leg-spinners like to 'give the ball plenty of air', to toss it up, hoping to deceive the batsman in the flight and cause him to be either stumped, or caught off a false stroke. Lewis clearly prefers a flatter trajectory. His last ball is a googly. But it's too short, and Fulton smacks the ball thankfully away to the leg-side boundary. The players leave the field. The Black Caps are 90 for 2 after 111 minutes batting, and in the box-seat.

Limited-overs cricket? Neville Cardus said to me it's like trying to play Beethoven on a banjo.

Bomber Wells,
quoted in
Runs in the Memory

Lunch break

IT HAS BEEN, for Tony and me, a very satisfactory morning's Test cricket. There were some quick wickets, some cavalier stroke play, but also determination, particularly from the newcomer, Fulton. After 3 for 2, 90 for 2 looks much healthier; the balance of power in the match has, for the moment, significantly shifted. This is part of the richness of the five-day Test match: because a Test match takes such a long time, all kinds of extra shifts and tilts in ascendancy become possible. In the first Test, the ascendancy was constantly seesawing as one side, then the other, gained the upper hand.

This leads us into a comparison of five-day Test cricket versus one-day, limited-overs cricket. I suggest that a Test match is the epic poem or five-act-play version of cricket. When it works, it has everything: high drama, reversals of fortune, endurance, aching disappointment, unlikely heroism, character writ large. It does literally 'test' the players to the utmost. Paul Fitzpatrick, writing in the *Guardian* in July 1981, after Ian Botham's batting and Bob Willis' bowling in the third Test at Headingley had given England an 'impossible' victory over Australia, exactly caught this grand, dramatic dimension:

> Only Test cricket could have produced such a fascinating plot as this; no other game could have allowed such an unlikely and outrageous swing of fortune as England experienced. Only a drama that is allowed to unfold over five days could permit such a twist in the plot so wild as to be unthinkable.

All the same, a Test match is not to everyone's taste. Because it takes so long it can sometimes be boring, like parts of *Paradise Lost* and *A Midsummer's Night's Dream*. But for the fanatic that is part of its appeal. Not, of course, that we want to be bored, but how liberating, how bold, to risk the dull and the slow in an ever-quickening world. The explosive moments burst out so much more vividly and memorably. The sudden decisive turn of a game carries an immensely greater charge than the fall of yet another wicket in a one-day, limited-overs match.

This is not to deny the attractions of the limited-overs game, both the established 50-overs-a-side version and the more recent 20-overs variety. This form of the game was seriously brought in at first-class level in the early 1960s – in the interests of 'brighter cricket' – and at international level a decade later. Now firmly entrenched, the limited-overs game has its own excitement and rewards. It encourages batsmen to go for their shots straight away; to watch an Adam Gilchrist, Virender Sehwag or Shahid Afridi hitting fours and sixes from the opening over is a delight.

Restrictions and handicaps have, as always, led to innovation. Batsmen have developed new shots, such as the chip over the infield on the on-side, pioneered in the late '70s by the New Zealand batsman Glenn Turner; also the fruitful, if sometimes ludicrous, reverse sweep.

Bowlers have also been forced to improvise. Faster bowlers have devised all kinds of disguised slower balls, from Glenn McGrath's split-finger delivery to Chris Cairns's rolled off-break. The fielding, too, is frequently electrically athletic. And the crowds usually attend en masse in a way they do only intermittently for Tests (and hardly at all for ordinary first-class matches).

If the equation between balls left and runs required is sufficiently tight, the conclusion to limited-overs games, at all levels, can be incredibly tense. It is then that nerve counts. Can the bowler avoid bowling wides and long hops, no balls and full tosses? Landing the ball in the block-hole, trying to york the batsman, is a good ploy, but the margin for error is very small. Can the batsman avoid mere slogging – which, even with a good eye, is usually a recipe for disaster – and find the inevitable gaps in the field?

Certain players have become one-day specialists. That was how my prep-school captain Woolmer first made it into the Kent and then England sides: as a highly economical medium-paced bowler who could also bat. Throughout the 1990s, the New Zealanders Gavin Larsen and Chris Harris were acknowledged one-day specialists: Larsen as the meanest of medium-pacers and Harris as both a batsman adept at resuscitating lost innings and a tantalisingly slow bowler able to apply a clamp on the opposition's scoring rate.

One of the most nerve-wracking limited-overs finishes I've seen was at the dawn of the one-day game. In 1963 I was among 25,000 spectators at Lord's who watched the first Gillette Cup knockout final. This was the competition's trial season at county level: 60 overs-a-side with a maximum of 15 overs per bowler. (300 was then considered a huge score. Now, off 50 overs, South Africa and Australia have both broken the 400-run barrier.)

The final was between Sussex and Worcestershire.

Graveney was playing for Worcestershire, and Snow, not yet a hero of mine, for Sussex. It was a chilly, murky September day but the pitch was taking spin, and things looked promising when Sussex were out for 168. Worcestershire, however, were only 133 when last man Bob Carter, the Galloping Major, went in. As a batsman, Carter was definitely in the Chris Martin class. Worcestershire had played badly. Graveney had made 29 but far too slowly. He even allowed Sussex's two part-time spinners to deliver 18 overs between them for 24 runs.

Dexter, the Sussex and England captain, had a much shrewder appreciation of limited-overs requirements. When the visibility began to fade (no stoppage for bad light back then, or floodlights as there would be now), he brought on Snow, held in reserve and very quick. Snow promptly took three wickets.

With Carter at the crease, it seemed all over. But he and the Worcestershire wicket-keeper Roy Booth, a reliable bat, started to make a stand. Booth worked the ball around. It was getting pretty dark. Booth and Carter stole singles. There were misfields. Ten runs were made. Fifteen. Twenty. Only 15 more needed, but only two overs left. This would now seem eminently gettable. Booth had to hit a couple of fours. Dexter placed all his fielders out on the boundary, except of course the wicket-keeper. At the time this was an unheard-of thing to do. My father was indignant. So was Booth. He held up play and slowly pointed out to the crowd each of the nine distant white figures. There was some applause, some booing at Dexter's tactics. But they worked. The Galloping Major was run out in the penultimate over, and Sussex won by 14 runs.

For a 13-year-old that game offered the allure of heroic failure, a feeling cricket regularly arouses in its followers. It was when New Zealander Lance Cairns hit Dennis Lillee and company for six sixes in a lost cause of a one-dayer against Australia in the early 1980s that he became a national icon.

The irony about one-day limited-overs cricket is that, although it can be very exciting, it can also, in its own way, be just as boring as the longer form of the game. If the side batting first scores a very low total, or a very high one, the result becomes a foregone conclusion, and of little further interest. The acid test is that it is almost impossible to recall more than a handful of one-day games in any detail. There are so many they quickly blur into each other. This is why some cynics refer to one-day cricket (and especially the 20-20 variety) as McCricket.

Another objection to one-day cricket might at first appear paradoxical. In a limited-overs game, the side that scores the most runs wins. Pure and simple. What's wrong with that? Nothing, except that there is no place for a draw. Naturally, a draw can be boring, but it can equally be thrilling. To hold out for a draw when the other side seems certain to win reveals qualities of technique, concentration, endurance which compel the imagination, which speak to us like stories of great escapes: Trevor Bailey and Willie Watson batting most of the final day at Lord's in 1953 to secure a draw against the Australian pace and spin of Ray Lindwall, Keith Miller, Bill Johnston, Alan Davidson, Richie Benaud and Doug Ring; the Australians 'Slasher' Mackay and Lindsay Kline holding out against Frank Worrell's West Indians in 1961. I still recall with a frisson how in 1967 Jim Jackson and I, the Wellington College last pair, held out for twenty minutes to draw a match against another public school.

The great cricket writer and radio commentator John Arlott registered the main problem with limited-overs cricket back in 1972. While appreciating its many merits, he spelt out its 'one unjustifiable deficiency':

> It must be a negation of the idea of cricket when a fielding side does better to restrict the opposing batsmen to 150 for no wicket than to bowl them all out for 151.

In its own terms, his point is irrefutable. However, the trouble with objections to one-day cricket is that they always smack of Golden Ageism. Cricket fanatics are especially prone to this form of nostalgia. 'The game's not the same' was probably already a *cri de cœur* back in 1628 when those ten men were fined a shilling each. It underlies Nyren's evergreen reminiscences of the Hambledon players of yesteryear. Lost youth is the key here. The cricketers of one's youth batted better and bowled faster than anyone else can or ever could. Everyone middle-aged or older has felt this, has felt as the late nineteenth century poet and Lancashire supporter Francis Thompson felt at Lord's: 'O my Hornby and my Barlow long ago!'

And speaking of nostalgia, it was my prep school which turned me into a real cricket fanatic. Cricket permeated the place. The headmaster, A.F. Bickmore — known to us boys as Mr Eric, from his second name, Frederick — had opened the batting for Oxford and Kent just after the First World War. Cricket writer R.C. Robertson-Glasgow described Bickmore at Oxford as 'a tall and stylish batsman with great power of stroke, and a fine fielder at short-leg, who favoured a large sun-hat.' School legend had it that if he hadn't had to take over the family school he would have gone on the 1924–25 MCC tour of Australia. He was a mild, grey man who taught Latin and was always sucking on an empty pipe.

Mr Eric's older brother, Mr Maurice, also taught Latin. He wore a pince-nez and had a temper like a time bomb. At evening prep he would pad around the silent room in his green slippers, tick-tick-tick — exploding if anyone dared to misbehave: 'What do you mean by it, you intolerable little mountebank!' The fact I was keen on cricket was useful: it meant he didn't often pick on me.

Nor, even more importantly, did most of the other boys.

It was Mr Eric's sons, Mr John and Mr Michael, who really ran the school. Mr John, another pipe-smoker, coached the First XI, although we all knew he wasn't much of a player. He had a lisp, a permanent five-o'clock shadow, and used hair oil. If you were a favourite of his, he would tickle you. Sometimes he tickled boys in bed before Lights Out.

On the whole, we liked Mr John and were afraid of Mr Michael. Mr Michael, younger, married, always called us 'child'. 'Come here, child,' he would say, rather like the crocodile in the Kipling story about how the elephant got its trunk. On the rare occasions he said, 'Well played, child', it was as though God himself was pleased with you. When he told me off one evening after my bath for being a bad sport, I felt the whole world had fallen apart. But it was also Mr Michael who, in May 1961, decided that since I was tall I might make a fast bowler. I was then in the under-elevens. A month later I was opening the bowling for the First XI and batting with Ussher.

In the summer term, we lived for cricket. Every break we would be out on the playground in our blue aertex shirts and grey shorts playing 'wogger', our home-grown version. In the evenings after tea, we were sent across the road to The Fields. Some boys built camps round the perimeter; others played ad hoc cricket matches, or practised in the four concrete nets next to the road.

Because of the concrete, we had to use cork balls instead of leather ones, which would soon have lost their casing. Sometimes Mr Eric would appear and, with his pipe as a diminutive bat, demonstrate a correct forward defensive. It was probably he who was responsible for the original laying of the nets back in 1926, and for the instant repair of the one hit by a German bomb in 1940.

In the winter of 2001, on a visit to England, my wife Belinda and I drove over to Tonbridge to have a look at my old school. It was early afternoon, the light already fading. We found the place all right: the street map in my head still worked. The many-windowed main building housing dormitories and classrooms, the red-roofed gym, the playground, the gardens, the extensive playing fields: they had all vanished. In their place sprawled a large, clearly rather desirable housing estate. The only relics were the bare concrete blocks of the practice nets across the road and a signpost on the road leading into the housing estate. 'Bickmore Way', it proclaimed.

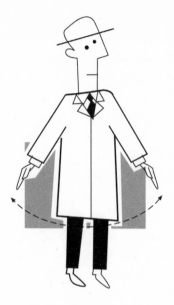

Umpire signal: dead ball

Shrewsbury to Bosanquet: 'That new ball of yours, Mr Bosanquet, is unfair.'

Ray Illingworth and Kenneth Gregory, *The Ashes*

Bosanquet to Shrewsbury: 'Not at all, Arthur. Merely immoral.'

Afternoon session

AFTER LUNCH it's Gayle bowling at the scoreboard end and Bradshaw at the other. Fleming takes a single off Gayle, and Fulton bats out the over. Bradshaw beats Fleming outside the off-stump, tempts him again, but Fleming leaves. Next ball, a little overpitched, he drives to the point boundary. Fulton patiently plays a maiden from Gayle. Fleming cuts and glances Bradshaw for a four and a three. He's picked up his pre-lunch tempo.

Fulton is also seeing the ball now and, after a cover-drive for four off Bradshaw, he hits Gayle for a couple of sixes over long-off and long-on to take him to 50.

It's been a good knock, and a timely one. He's looked secure throughout and answered those who would have liked to see Mathew Sinclair at number 3. (Tony and I think Sinclair, rather than Scott Styris, should bat number six but that's another story.)

A tall man, Fulton has a high backlift and likes to drive. He seems a natural candidate for the yorker. That was how the West Indian quick bowlers of the 1970s, Michael Holding, Andy Roberts and Wayne Daniel, regularly disposed of the giraffe-like England captain Tony Greig, who had foolishly promised to make the West Indies 'grovel'. But Roberts and co were in a different league from the current Windies' attack.

Then, suddenly, after punching Bradshaw for four, Fleming in the same over pushes at a good length ball and ... is dropped at second slip. It's another bad miss – the third to date in this innings. That would have made it 140 for 3 and improved Bradshaw's figures, which currently stand at 12 overs, 1 maiden, 67 runs and 1 wicket to 12–1–67–2.

Gayle, the off-spinner, after being hit for those sixes, is given a rest, and the leg-spinner Lewis comes back on. This is a good move by Chanderpaul. Gayle's job was to keep the runs down, and he was failing to do it. Lewis is a reasonable gamble because New Zealanders don't get much practice playing leg-spin (see figure 4).

Figure 4 **Leg-spin and off-spin**

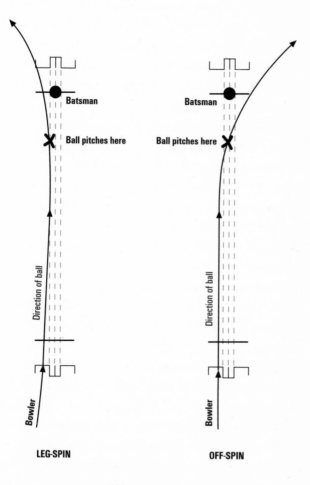

LEG-SPIN   OFF-SPIN

| | | = line of wicket

I remember the first leg-spinner I ever played with. He was a boy at prep school called Gourlay. We were friends, but also cricketing rivals. I wanted to bowl as fast as possible but I was fascinated by Gourlay's ability, when bowling to a right-hander, to make the ball spin sharply anticlockwise from right to left, leg-side to off-side. While I would point the seam towards the batsman, trying to make it swing in the air or 'cut' off the pitch, Gourlay would hold it crossways, lightly gripped between his thumb and first two fingers, with a gap between these and his third finger and little finger, which would be tucked up towards his palm. It was those last two fingers and his 'cocked' wrist which gave the ball its decisive twist or 'tweak' as he released it. When he pitched the ball in the right place, he could be devastating.

Leg-spinners divide into 'rippers' and 'rollers'. Rippers are often less accurate and can be expensive, but do give the ball a sharp tweak and often take wickets. Rollers, as the term implies, tend to roll the wrist over in delivery, rather than giving it a fierce twist. They are generally accurate but don't spin the ball much.

Back in the 1950s in New Zealand, Jack Alabaster and Alex Moir were both effective purveyors of leg-spin. Indeed, Alabaster took crucial wickets in New Zealand's first ever Test win (against the West Indies) in 1956 and their second Test win (against South Africa) in 1962. But today you rarely see leg-spin in local domestic cricket. The last leg-spinner to play in a Test for New Zealand was the ill-fated Greg Loveridge in 1996; he was injured during that one appearance and never actually bowled a ball.

Lewis is definitely a roller. Although he has only ever taken one Test wicket, he's not a bad bet this afternoon. He drops on a length straight away and is tidy if not particularly challenging. In fact, he manages two maidens in a row before Fleming hits him high for four.

The great contemporary leg-spinner is the Australian Shane Warne. Tony likes to claim Warne is the greatest leg-spinner ever, and few would argue. When he needs to, Warne can still achieve big turn, even on wickets like this, which don't offer much assistance. In his younger days, that was Warne's trump card – that and the fact that, unlike other modern leg-spinners, he bowled to hit the wicket.

Any extended conversation with Tony about Shane Warne tends to include some reference to a bamboozled Mike Gatting being bowled by Warne's very first ball in a Test in England in 1993 – a huge leg-spinner which pitched outside Gatting's leg-stump and hit off-stump. Nowadays, we agree, Warne's real threat is his range of variations and the mind games he plays with batsmen – or gets them to play with themselves. In addition to variously spun leg-breaks, Warne has a slider, which doesn't spin but hurries on to the batsman, often creating an lbw. He does have a googly but doesn't bowl it much any more, perhaps wisely: it was bowling googlies that did for Richie Benaud's shoulder in the early 1960s, and in the 1930s did for the English leg-spinner Ian Peebles — although in Peebles's case he ended up unable to bowl anything *except* googlies.

The googly was invented by the English cricketer B.J.T. Bosanquet in the 1890s. Australians still sometimes call it a 'bosie', in honour of its originator. Put simply, a googly is an off-break delivered with a leg-break action — the ball coming out of the back of the hand. In other words, the ball is delivered with a clockwise spin and veers in the opposite direction to what the batsman's expecting. In its day the googly was as remarkable an innovation as the 'Little Farmer' Lamborn's discovery of the off-break in the eighteenth century. (Richard Nyren said of Lamborn that his 'comprehension did not equal the speed of lightning' and he had to be taught exactly where to pitch the ball so that it would actually go on to hit the wicket.)

There are various accounts of how the far from simple Bosanquet developed his 'immoral' delivery. In one story it evolved from his playing 'twisty-grab' on the billiard table and finding that if a ball were spun from right to left and released out of the back of the hand, it would turn from the left to the right. In another version, he was spinning tennis balls in the garden. Bosanquet's first first-class wicket with his strange new delivery was in 1900. The ball apparently bounced four times on its way to the perplexed batsman, who was stumped.

Although often erratic, Bosanquet twice won Test matches against Australia with his baffling invention.

New Zealand can legitimately lay claim to having christened the googly. At least, the earliest known printed use of the term in a cricketing sense was in the *New Zealand Times* of 19 January 1903. Bosanquet was a member of the 1902–03 MCC tour of New Zealand, and the match report mentioned that Bosanquet's 'googely ones' were relished by the batsmen. In *Cricket Across the Seas*, his published account of the tour, 'Plum' Warner, the MCC captain, alluded to 'Bosanquet's slow "googlies" as they are called in New Zealand', and suggested the word meant 'something weird, freakish, almost uncanny'.

I enjoy reminding Tony that the great Australian leg-spin and googly bowler of the late 1920s and '30s, Clarrie Grimmett, was a New Zealander by origin. Yes, he replies, but he had to move to Oz, didn't he, to become a great leg-spinner? There is no arguing with this. The softer, grassier New Zealand pitches, like those in England, don't generally reward leg-spin and googly bowlers; they suit seam and swing bowlers better. Leg-spin and googly bowlers tend to thrive in hotter countries, such as Australia and the Indian subcontinent, with harder and/or flatter pitches.

The googly is not the only delivery with a strange history. There's also the chinaman. This refers to a ball bowled by a slow left-arm bowler and spinning into a right-handed batsman as an off-break. It is, in effect, the mirror-image of a right-arm bowler's leg-break and has its equivalent googly out of the back of the hand. Again, there are different versions of how the chinaman got its name. One version has it that when the early 1930s' English all-rounder Walter Robins was stumped off Ellis Achong, a West Indian slow left-armer of Chinese descent, he exclaimed, 'Fancy getting out to a bloody chinaman!' Another version assigns the remark to the Yorkshireman Maurice Leyland.

In its way even more uncanny than either the googly or the chinaman is the doosra, bowled by the Sri Lankan Muttiah Muralitharan. This is a leg-break delivered with an off-break action.

At the drinks break, New Zealand are 150 for 2. The early afternoon can sometimes turn into a flat period, but not today: 60 since lunch, run-a-minute stuff. Fleming on 86, Fulton on 54.

Umpire signal: no ball

Together join'd in cricket's manly toil.

Lord Byron,
'Childish
Recollections'

Drinks break

DURING THE BREAK Tony and I talk about what cricket has meant to us. I tell him about my cricket-mad prep school, and how the game was a way to gain acceptance – and if you bowled fast, people left you alone. The same was true at my English public school, Wellington College. There the real heroes were the 'rugger-buggers', striding around the colonnades ten foot tall and five foot wide, in their tasselled caps and orange and black striped scarves. But opening the bowling for the First XI came a reasonable second and if, like me, you were bookish, it stopped people calling you a pseud, at least to your face.

Did I ever tell you how cricket stopped me being a wog? asks Tony in return. In the part of Sydney where I grew up, if you were known to be of Italian extraction, or Greek or Polish, you were a wog. In fact, everyone who wasn't Anglo or Irish or Aborigine was a wog. And a name like Schirato was a dead giveaway. When I was 18 or 19, I was fielding at square-leg one day, right next to the square-leg umpire, who was a player from the opposing side. (You know, the way you act as your own umpires.) We'd played against each other before, and this guy knew me and my name and that I'd been scoring a lot of runs. And he suddenly said, about someone else from another team entirely: 'He's a real fucking wog!' And at that moment I knew that I wasn't a wog any more; I was okay.

There is no matching a story like this and I don't try. But it sets me thinking about when I first arrived in New Zealand. It was the winter of 1981, and within weeks the country was up to its shin-pads in the Springbok tour. I was against the tour, and in support of those trying to stop it. But what really fascinated me, I tell Tony, was hearing that many of the demonstrators carried transistors while marching outside the grounds where the games were being played. Their protest was absolutely genuine, but they did just want to keep track of the score.

Tony laughs. The conversation swings back to cricket and how it's always been full of eccentrics and oddballs, people like C. Aubrey Smith, the 1930s Hollywood actor who, in an earlier incarnation, captained England and was known as 'Round-the-Corner Smith' on account of his peculiar run up to the wicket. And the England captain Mike Brearley, who, while waiting for Jeff Thomson to begin his inordinately long run, used to hum the opening of Beethoven's first Rasumovsky Quartet to steady his nerves. And then there's 'Typhoon' Tyson, my hero at five, who would apparently recite Wordsworth as he plodded slowly back to the start of his equally long run. What about Derek Randall, Tony chips in, that time the Indian crowd slow-hand-clapped him, and he dropped his bat, and knelt down and lifted his hands in prayer?

Cricket and its oddballs have a way of following you. At Hong Kong University in the 1970s, I had the desk that had been used by the poet Edmund Blunden during his time as professor in the English department in the 1950s and '60s. Like his friend and fellow World War I poet Siegfried Sassoon, Blunden was a fanatical cricketer. *His* oddity was that he never wore gloves when batting.

During my Hong Kong stint I played in the university side, a mongrel bunch of English, Australians, Kiwis and Indians; the only criterion seemed to be that you had once attended a university somewhere. One of my fellow players was a one-armed, ex-international lacrosse player called Terry. On first encountering Terry, opposing sides would anticipate an easy victim, until he began hitting them for some of the biggest sixes I've ever seen. Some years later in New Zealand, I regularly played against a guy with an artificial leg. He had a good eye and often made runs against us. I found the trick, bowling to him, was to keep the ball pitched right up – as near to yorker length as possible without offering up a juicy full toss.

But Tony's mind is on things other than prosthetic limbs. You know how everyone goes on about how homo-erotic rugby is, he says suddenly. Has it ever struck you that cricket is every bit as sexual in its codified way? What could be more phallic than stumps and bats? And as for balls... Remember that Monty Python sketch – what was it? 'Polanski's cricket match', something like that. It has this wonderful shot of the bowler slowly and lasciviously rubbing the ball on the inside groin part of his trousers. I ask you: isn't that what every fast bowler does to keep the shine on the new ball? 'The Auto-erotics of Cricket': someone should write a paper on it, he suggests.

Someone probably has, I reply, not to mention the underlying implications of 'ball tampering'. All that roughing up of one side of the ball to create reverse swing. Now there's a PhD topic: 'Transgressive Sexuality and Reverse Swing'. Or, says Tony, what about England captain Mike Atherton trying to make one side of the ball heavier by applying dirt from his pockets? Freud would have had a field day with that.

Umpire signal: leg-bye

The delicate thuggery and stylishly reserved ostentation of a cricket test match.

Ian Wedde,
The Viewing Platform

Afternoon session, continued

TONY AND I, despite our affection for the bank, have moved to the R. A. Vance Stand. We have passes and it seems a shame not to use them. We are reasonably high up, looking down from behind mid-on or third man, depending which end is bowling.

Edwards is on again from our end, down wind. The crowd's attention quickens. So far in the innings he has bowled only seven overs. Since he has been the West Indies' main strike bowler on this tour, his relatively undemanding workload presents a small mystery. Why no initial burst straight after lunch? asks Tony.

That would have been logical before the batsmen got re-established. Perhaps he's carrying an injury, I suggest. Edwards is known to be a bit injury-prone, and we remember that he was stamping his foot as though in some discomfort in his first spell. Maybe Chanderpaul is nursing him.

Alternatively, Tony and I speculate, Chanderpaul may have had a cunning plan which backfired. It's always fun trying to second-guess a captain's intentions. The cunning plan (not all that cunning really) could have been to 'buy' a wicket or two with his spinners Gayle and Lewis – as he would have done, had catches been held. Then Chanderpaul could have thrown in a fresh Edwards to make a decisive breakthrough.

Back in the real world, Fleming marks out a fresh guard. Edwards has two slips, a gully, mid-off and, like Bradshaw, a fielder deep on the point boundary on the off-side. Fleming off-drives his first ball from Edwards sumptuously for four. His score is now 90. He's in the nervous nineties, as they're often called. This is one of those moments in a day's play when a player nears a milestone, and character stands out in sharp relief. Fleming is faced with a couple of options. He can continue to play in the expansive, attacking vein he has adopted so successfully so far in his innings, or he can simply defend and see Edwards off. (He'll probably have only a four-over spell.) Or, a middle option, he can cut out the big shots and work the ones and twos.

Fleming has never made a Test 100 at the Basin. Now he's just past his previous top score here of 88. It's a knowledgeable crowd; many of them will know this. There is a definite air of expectation.

Edwards' second ball is a slower one; Fleming digs it out. Off the fourth ball, he pushes a single. 155 for 2, Fleming 91. Perhaps he is taking the middle option after all. Fulton plays out the over. Edwards has kept every ball pitched well up, nothing at all short.

Lewis continues at the other end, keeping it tight. He has a long-on back for Fleming, encouraging him to hit in the air. Third ball, Fleming takes a quick single on the off-side. 92 now, eight runs to go.

Edwards again to Fleming. The first ball is short and straight. Fleming pulls convulsively. There are four fielders on the leg-side: mid-on, short mid-wicket, deep square-leg and long-leg. He is late on the shot. The ball hits high on the bat. It could go anywhere. A shortish square-leg could have snaffled it comfortably, but there's no one there. Fleming and Fulton jog through for a single. Hearts return from mouths to their ordinary position.

A missed opportunity there, Tony says, meaning Fleming missed out on an easy boundary. Clearly Fleming is not going to be content to inch his way to his century. Against Edwards at least he is going to keep attacking. Some bowlers bring out this reaction in a batsman. They get under the skin somehow. Tony points out how adept Shane Warne is at this kind of mind game, how when he's bowling there's always needle, always a bit of edge. Take me on, he seems to say, tossing the ball up high, bet you can't. Edwards seems to have an equivalent effect on Fleming. There was that missed chance off the ill-judged hook before lunch. Now this. Part of me wants Fleming to carry on in this swashbuckling fashion; another part just wants him to get his 100 any old how.

Edwards fires in more short balls at Fulton, which he copes with competently enough. Edwards' last over was full; this one so far has been short, rising chest-high — the quickest at 146 kilometres per hour is a no ball. Look out for the yorker, Tony says. Fulton obviously is, because the last two balls of the over are attempted yorkers. He strokes the first for four through the vacant mid-on and takes a single off the second, an attempted slower ball which ends up as a full toss. 163 for 2, Fleming still on 93. Lewis bowls a maiden to Fulton; one ball beats him outside the off-stump.

Back to the Edwards–Fleming duel. Edwards goes around the wicket now. He did this before lunch, when he had Fleming dropped at long-leg. It can be a good move against a left-handed batsman: the ball tends to angle into the player, cramping him for room in which to play his shots. The first ball, however, is a long-hop outside off-stump, one of Fleming's favourite areas to score. He plays a delicate late-cut, a dab really, between second slip and gully for four. 167 for 2, Fleming 97.

Second ball. Edwards strains for extra pace. The ball is again shortish, but this time it does angle back into Fleming. Seeing the length, he again shapes to guide it down to fine third-man. But as the ball moves back on to him he ends up merely defending, rather inelegantly. The umpire's arm goes out; it was a no ball. If Fleming had heard the call in time, he could have had a free hit.

After two short ones, the next ball is full, another attempted yorker. Fleming, tempted to drive, finds the ball not quite there and has to dig it out. No run. Waiting.

The next ball is again short, and a bit wide outside the off-stump. Fleming cuts hard and high. This is the shot that brought him those three consecutive sixes in the one-day game at Napier. It's a certain four, possibly a six. Except that he has picked out Dwayne Bravo on the edge of the wide point boundary. Fleming backs away, backs away, his eyes following the path of the ball. Bravo takes the catch without fuss just inside the boundary rope. Fleming's head goes down.

Perhaps, Tony suggests, that was Chanderpaul's real plan against Fleming all along: the short, rising ball outside the off-stump, which Fleming would not be able to resist, and which he would be likely to hit in the air with that sliced uppercut stroke of his. With Bradshaw the plan had failed, because he was too slow and the ball sat up at a comfortable height. That's where Edwards' extra pace and bounce made all the difference. Edwards was the only bowler against whom Fleming had looked uncertain. He had earned his wicket. New Zealand 168 for 3. A partnership between Fleming and Fulton of 165. West Indies are high-fiving, jubilant. Fleming out for 97, scored off 131 balls in a fraction over three hours, with 15 fours and one six. Tony and I watch him leave the field. His disappointment, like the crowd's, is palpable.

Tony and I are disappointed too. Fleming deserved a hundred. To watch him bat is always an aesthetic experience. The same is true of Brian Lara, and of Sachin Tendulkar, the Indian cricketer who holds the record for the most Test centuries, and was equally true of Tom Graveney and Martin Crowe. Crowe was sometimes accused (in New Zealand but never overseas) of being a bit of a prima donna. This reflected a complete misunderstanding of what made him tick as a batsman. Cricket writer and former selector Don Neely got it right when he told sports writer Joseph Romanos, author of the unauthorised biography *Martin Crowe: Tortured Genius*: 'It's not enough [for Crowe] to score a century. He wants it to be a classic innings, a perfect innings. He's one of the few batsmen you could imagine scoring a test century and being unhappy with his innings.' This is confirmed by Crowe's autobiography, *Out on a Limb*, in which he gives a sharp inside view of the experience of Test cricket. Fleming is the Black Caps' natural successor to Crowe. I suggest this to Tony, only to find that while I've been meditating on cricketing aesthetes he has been trying to initiate me into the mysteries of baseball.

Figure 5 **Edwards' field to Fleming**

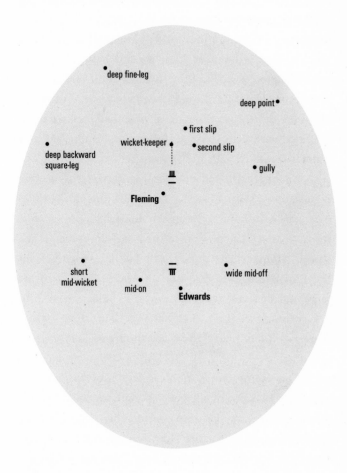

Edwards' field placement when he had Fleming caught on the
deep point boundary for 97.

Nathan Astle appears. There are three balls in the over to go. I remind Tony that Edwards shook Astle up in the one-dayers with some short-pitched stuff. This brings him back from the world of knuckle balls and first bases. Edwards bounces Astle second ball. Astle takes evasive action, cuts his third ball for four. Lewis bowls another maiden to Fulton. Edwards bounces Fulton and hits him on the shoulder. The next ball looks like an intended yorker, the obvious follow-up; Fulton, unfazed, collects three through mid-wicket.

Astle is in restrained-but-purposeful mode, as he often is nowadays. With Fleming gone, he's the side's senior batsman. Astle used to be in the 'master blaster' mould, ready to attack the bowling almost as soon as he'd taken guard. Many in the crowd will fondly remember his thrilling 222 against England in March 2002, with 28 fours and 11 sixes, made off only 168 balls, a record for a Test double century. But that was then. Now Astle is more careful, prepared to occupy the crease and graft for his runs.

All the same, you'd never group him in with the 'thinking' players, those who, by applying their intelligence, turn themselves into considerably more than the sum of their parts. Former New Zealand captain Jeremy Coney remains the pre-eminent local example. I remember him explaining to me once how he played the English fast bowler Bob Willis. Willis didn't swing or move the ball much, but he bowled a very tight off-stump line and mostly relied on steep bounce to create chances behind the wicket (like a quicker version of Chris Martin). Coney's solution was to take an off-stump guard: anything to the off, he left alone; anything straight, he played down or tucked away to leg. 'Look in *Wisden* and see how often he got me out,' he said. Almost never is the answer. Coney also told me that on one tour of the subcontinent, the players suffered so badly from Delhi belly that they were all issued with nappies to wear on the field.

Astle is soon accumulating: a single here, a two there. When Edwards bounces him again he once more ducks, rather than risk the hook or pull he would undoubtedly have unleashed in a one-day game or earlier in his career. It's not that long until tea. He's apparently happy to play himself in, let his partner unleash the big shots. As soon as Powell replaces Edwards after a short, expensive but successful burst, Fulton hits him for six over mid-wicket, followed by a single to put the Black Caps in the lead. Powell is looser than he was before lunch and Astle, too, starts to take toll, with a sliced four and a glanced three. A single each off Lewis, and it's tea.

New Zealand 207 for 3, a lead of 15 with 7 wickets left. A healthy position. They have kept up the momentum with 117 runs since lunch. The only wicket to fall has been Fleming's. Lewis has bowled 10 overs for 16 runs. No one seems to have reliably picked his googly, but it hasn't turned enough to cause problems.

You can either have sex before cricket or after cricket – the fundamental fact is that cricket must be there at the centre of things.

Harold Pinter,
'Quote ... Unquote'

Tea break

TONY DECIDES to take a walk. I stay put; my mind is still on Fleming's dismissal. His tussle with Edwards has undoubtedly been the highlight of the day so far. The fact it was played out over several sessions added to the drama. Fleming treated the other bowlers with some disdain, particularly Bradshaw, but the real battle was always with Edwards, against whom he never looked entirely comfortable.

To watch an encounter like that gradually develop, to sense its growing intensity, to be caught up in the crowd's feeling, to become part of the rhythm of the play is one of the special rewards of watching cricket live. This is where C. L. R. James seems right in thinking of cricket as a kind of art form, like theatre or sculpture. In cricket, he argues in *Beyond a Boundary*, 'the significant form at its most unadulterated is permanently present. It is known, expected, recognised and enjoyed by tens of thousands of spectators. Cricketers call it style.'

This is not to knock some of the other ways of experiencing a cricket match. Over the decades television has provided me with some of my most intense cricketing experiences, both with Tests and one-dayers. Radio, too. The soundtrack of my teens was a mélange of Bob Dylan, John Arlott, the Rolling Stones, T. S. Eliot and Brian Johnston. Radio has always been the medium for the quick wisecrack or *double entendre*. Only on radio could Brian Johnston have got away with his absolutely deadpan, 'The bowler's Holding, the batsman's Willey.' It was Arlott, inevitably, who delivered my favourite quip on radio. On New Zealand's 1969 tour of England, one of the team members was the medium-pacer Bob Cunis. During one Test, along with thousands of other listeners, I heard John Arlott utter his cheeky *bon mot*: 'And here comes Cunis – neither one thing nor the other...'

These days, my summer wouldn't be the same without Jeremy Coney's witty, well-informed commentaries. While watching the game on television with the sound off, I listen to Coney on the radio. He always has some theory to try out and, like Arlott, manages to bring the whole scene to life while providing the expert technical analysis that real addicts never get tired of.

My late father-in-law Dick knew how to 'suffer' his cricket, as Arlott would say. Up at the family bach at Lake Rotoma, everything was kept as simple as *Swallows and Amazons*: no electricity, cooking on a wood range, washing in the lake, long-drop. But Dick always made sure he brought a small radio with plenty of batteries, and away from the main building he had a corrugated-iron-roofed lean-to, known as Lord's. Reception, of course, was lousy: the trick was to intertwine the aerial into the wire fence. But I spent many afternoons, and several late nights, at Lord's with Dick and my brother-in-law Garry, listening to cricket matches being played in New Zealand and overseas. Dick would sit in his blue beret with his legs crossed, concentrating intently as the commentary hummed and faded, alternately groaning and cheering according to the state of play.

Belinda (who had inherited his passion) and I took Dick to the Basin Reserve several times. We were there in 1999 when, on his debut, Mathew Sinclair scored a double hundred against the West Indies. Before he had scored a run, Sinclair got an inside edge (sometimes called a 'French cut', or 'Harrow drive') which narrowly missed his wicket and went to the boundary for four. He could so easily have played it on, as How did earlier today. This takes me back to Fleming and one of cricket's perennial fascinations: the way the game both reveals and conceals character. Was it bad luck that got Fleming out yet again between 50 and 100? Or some self-destructive impulse? If so, is he perhaps a secret neurotic? He always looks relaxed, unruffled. And when required he can grind it out, if so ugly a term can be applied to so elegant a player. But who knows what inner demons Fleming may deal with?

Take my prep-school hero Ussher. Watching Ussher bat, you might have assumed he was a confident extrovert. In reality he was intensely superstitious, and had various personal rituals to bring him luck. One was to make sure he was bowled or caught in the practice game or net we always had the evening before a school match. Personal superstitions and rituals are common among cricketers. On the morning of the Flower Show match, Siegfried Sassoon has his young alter ego use the previous day's cricket reports in the newspaper as a kind of horoscope to predict his own performance; his system is based on the scores of players with the same initials as himself. I can identify with this: for a whole season, I checked the scores of a Hampshire player called Barnard, simply because he had once scored 82 on the same day that I'd scored 28.

Many cricketers, particularly English ones, are superstitious about 'Nelson' (a score of 111) and its multiples. This is said to derive from Admiral Nelson of Trafalgar, possessor of one arm, one eye and, supposedly, one testicle. When a team or a player is on 'Nelson', everyone has to keep their feet off the floor. The rotund English umpire David Shepherd always stood on one leg when the score reached 'Nelson' and would remain stork-like until the fateful number was passed. The Australians, however, are more bothered by 87 because it's 13 away from a hundred.

Ussher and Fleming are certainly on stand-by for my World Neurotics XI. I carry around in my head an ever-changing list, a combination of real players and cricket-mad poets. Currently keeping wicket is the constantly yapping 'Jack' Russell (Gloucestershire and England). The likeable 'flat-track bully' Graeme Hick (Worcestershire and England) bats at three. He has recently scored his 130th first-class century, and now stands eighth in the all-time table, so he has to be exceptionally good. Yet, for some reason, presumably 'a bit of static in the old head', he never really made it at Test level.

The tearful Kim Hughes is in, perhaps the only Australian; he wept openly at the media conference at which he resigned the captaincy – an unheard-of show of emotion. Also the moody John Snow; he could talk poetry with Siegfried Sassoon in the outfield.

Snow and Richard Hadlee (Nottinghamshire and New Zealand) could open the bowling. Hadlee's selection is based on his OSS (Obsessive Statistics Syndrome) and his highly strung batting. In the 1980s, Hadlee deliberately set himself specific bowling targets to lift his often flagging motivation and maintain his performance at peak level. He might use the approaching holy grail of

300 Test wickets, say, or a designated number of wickets he aimed to take in a Test series. As a medium-to-fast right-arm bowler, Hadlee had a perfectly grooved action and was metronomically accurate. A wilder side showed itself in his often big-hitting left-handed batting.

Poor manic-depressive Harold Gimblett (Somerset and England) opens the innings, partnered by the recently retired Mark Richardson (New Zealand), who started out as a promising slow left-armer but gave up because of the 'yips' (extreme nervousness) and turned himself into a Test opener with an average of 44.

Derek Randall (Nottinghamshire and England) is another must. He was a brilliantly athletic fielder with huge feet. A natural clown, he celebrated England's regaining of the Ashes in 1977 with an exuberant cartwheel. He was an exciting but often nervous batsman, who drove opposing sides to distraction by constantly geeing himself up while he batted. 'Come, Rags,' he'd say, 'Concentrate. Only five minutes more and it's only half an hour 'til tea.'

Going back much further, there's Fred Tate (Sussex and England), father of the famous 1920s' England bowler Maurice Tate. Fred was a handy county bowler brought into the 1902 Test against Australia at Old Trafford, it is said, on a selectorial whim. Fred dropped a crucial catch on the boundary, went in last man with eight runs to win, had to go off for rain, snicked a four, and was then comprehensively bowled. Over a hundred years later that defeat is still referred to as 'Tate's Match'. If that's not enough to make you neurotic, I don't know what is.

Cricket fanatics love imaginary XIs. Childish but true. An Erotics XI would be fun. The nucleus might be built around real Test players such as 'Guy the Gorilla' Ian Botham, swashbuckling Percy Chapman, 'Brylcreem Boy' Denis Compton, Mike ('The Barmaid') Gatting, playboy Imran Khan, cavalier Keith Miller, quixotic Gary Sobers and irrepressible Shane Warne.

But there could also be a place for pin-up poets Lord Byron and Rupert Brooke. Byron played for Harrow against Eton in 1805 – with a runner because of his club foot. According to his account he scored a creditable eleven notches (runs) in the first innings and seven in the second. The surviving scorebook, probably equally unreliable, gives his scores as 7 and 2. Brooke was in the Rugby School XI in 1906, as a bowler and 'safe catch'. His end-of-season write-up – 'a slow bowler who at times kept a good length and puzzled the batsmen' – might also apply to his poetry.

And there should certainly be an Erotics spot for the mysterious MCC cricketer 'R', who was on the boat to New Zealand in 1906, and by whose 'firm hands' the 18-year-old Katherine Mansfield said she would like to be strangled. Tony's return jolts me out of this rather disturbing reverie as the players reappear on the field for the evening session.

A game
about which

you can know
very little

and say
anything

and be right
Brian Turner, *sooner or later.*
'Cricket'

Evening session

THE BLACK CAPS resume on 207 for 3, a lead of 15. Tony and I reckon that another 100 or so in the remaining two hours is probably the objective. Powell continues from the R. A. Vance Stand end to Fulton. So far Fulton has hardly put a foot wrong, but now, off the very first ball after tea, he waves his bat at a short-pitched ball outside the off-stump, doesn't move his feet and is caught by the wicket-keeper, Denesh Ramdin, for 75. It's 207 for 4. He hung his bat out to dry, observes Tony. We smile at the aptness of the old cricketing cliché and in mutual disappointment at Fulton's abrupt departure. This is exactly the kind of situation which often happens just before or just after an interval: one lapse in concentration and it's all over.

A small buzz goes around the ground. Attention quickens. Scott Styris walks to the wicket. This is a significant moment. New Zealand have only a slender lead. Two quick wickets now and the balance of power will have swung back decisively the West Indies' way.

Tony starts to spin a context around this innings of Styris's. In the first innings of the first Test, Styris scored a vital century. But in the second innings Edwards quickly hit him on the helmet, 'rattling his cage' as the commentators like to say. When batsmen are hit like that, they usually react in one of two ways: they concentrate on defence until the effects have worn off, or go instantly on the attack in an attempt to reassert themselves. In the first Test Styris took the second option, and within minutes he was brilliantly caught off another of Edwards' bouncers on the square-leg boundary. Had Bradshaw not caught the ball at full stretch above his head, it would have gone for six. You could say it was bad luck or, as Tony and I think, Styris was shaken up and suckered out.

Chanderpaul and his bowlers will remember this. They'll also remember that Styris later complained publicly about the lack of concern the Windies showed when he was hit. Powell isn't as quick as Edwards, but we reckon Styris won't be getting many balls to drive. Sure enough, his first ball from Powell is short. Styris pulls compulsively, mistimes his shot; the ball goes to mid-on. Two balls later, he's beaten outside the off-stump.

This is not promising. The wicket has certainly perked Powell up. He was a bit shambolic before tea, not properly following through the crease in his delivery stride. Now his action is suddenly smoother, everything's clicking. It's as though he has a new lease of life. This often happens when fast bowlers get wickets. One second they're looking ragged and reluctant, then suddenly it's as though they're a different player, bowling a yard or two quicker, and expecting something to happen with every ball.

Now surely, Tony says, Chanderpaul must bring on Edwards and test the new batsman with pace at both ends. But no, it is Lewis again as it was before tea. This is bizarre, and Chanderpaul's handling of his bowlers in general has been hard to fathom. The West Indies are momentarily in control; this is the time to strike. A Fleming or a Ponting or a Brearley would certainly not hesitate. A captain needs to intervene, to try things. Chanderpaul is too passive, too willing to let the game drift.

Lewis to Astle. Astle drives the first ball, a flighted delivery, through the covers for four. He then quietly plays out the over.

Back to Styris. Powell pitches up, and Styris drives him straight for four. The third ball is a bouncer, which he leaves. The fourth is also short. This time Styris can't resist the temptation, and pulls it successfully through mid-wicket – four. The fifth ball is well up just outside his off-stump. Styris is drawn into the shot, gets an edge, and is nonchalantly caught at second slip. As easy as that. 219 for 5, Styris out for 8.

The crowd is thoroughly awake. Two quick wickets. Surely Chanderpaul must replace Lewis with Edwards now.

While Styris wanders off, I start to tell Tony about Penny Kinsella, the New Zealand international whom I once had the good fortune to play with in the mid 1990s. She was known for playing the hook shot compulsively. I certainly remember her unleashing it on several quite pacey male bowlers in that match; they looked shaken.

And then there was David Steele – 'Stainless', as he was inevitably known. Steady English county batsmen who play for unfashionable counties don't usually get noticed, but Steele did. For over a decade, he had made good but unnoticed runs in a so-so Northants side. Then suddenly, in the summer of 1975, he was picked for the second Test against Australia at Lord's. England were just back from Australia, having been pulverised by the speed of Lillee and Thomson and thumped 4–1. When they were again destroyed by the same duo in the first Test in England, Tony Greig was made captain, and it was he who called for the 33-year-old.

'Stainless', batting number three, was in almost at once on the opening morning. With his usual plodding gait, rimless glasses and iron-grey hair poking out from under his tilted-up cap, he cut a rather improbable figure. 'Who have we here?' Thomson is supposed to have said. 'Groucho Marx?' But, wonderfully, Steele came off. He got 50. More runs in the second innings. An average of 60 for the series. The following year, he scored a century off the mighty West Indies' attack and played solidly in a losing side. But, although he went on in county cricket until 1984, those two summers of 1975 and 1976 marked the beginning and end of his Test career.

Your point being? asks Tony. What indeed was my point – except that I always enjoy telling Steele's story? The point, I reply, is that the West Indies worked out that Steele, for all his adhesive forward defensive, was a compulsive hooker – like Andrew Hilditch in England in 1985, I add, keen to get my own back. Always caught at fine- or long-leg, wasn't it? Don't mention Hilditch, says Tony with a sigh. Please don't mention Hilditch.

By now Brendon McCullum has arrived at the wicket and seen off the last ball of Powell's over. But still no Edwards at the other end. McCullum, like a lot of wicket-keepers, is a busy batsman, quick on his feet, and he has soon broken his duck. Against Powell and Lewis, he and Astle rarely look in trouble, although Astle still doesn't seem to be picking Lewis's googly.

McCullum hits a couple of fours off Powell, then a third. He's on 23 and the partnership is already worth 27 when he hooks at a high bouncer from Powell, gets a faint touch, and is very well caught by the leaping Ramdin. 246 for 6. A lead of only just over 50: another wicket now and the Windies will be right back in the game. The Black Caps are badly missing the recently retired Chris Cairns. He's been the best New Zealand all-rounder since John Reid in the 1950s and '60s. Like Jacques Kallis of South Africa and Andrew Flintoff of England, Cairns could turn a match with either bat or ball. His absence leaves a gaping hole in the middle-order.

With Styris and Steele in mind, I find myself telling Tony about the terrifying hour and a half's battering John Edrich and Brian Close took from Andy Roberts, Michael Holding, Wayne Daniel and Vanburn Holder at Old Trafford in 1976. I watched this on television. Close, who had started his erratic Test career in 1949 at the age of 18, was 45. Edrich was 39. No helmets; variable bounce; very fast bowling. They were both repeatedly hit on the body, and came off the field covered in bruises, undefeated. How one or both of them wasn't killed I'll never know. It was the gutsiest thing I've ever seen on a cricket field. It was also sickening and completely crazy. Like bodyline, observes Tony, watching to see how I'll react.

Yes, like bodyline. Bodyline: the shame of English cricket, the ultimate example of cricket being 'not cricket'. It was English captain Douglas Jardine's answer to the genius of Don Bradman in Australia, 1932–33: pack the leg-side with an inner and outer ring of fielders and get Larwood and Voce to bowl flat out at anywhere between the batsmen's chest and head. It worked, because Larwood, in particular, was a great bowler and very quick. But bodyline was also profoundly wrong. As the Australian captain Bill Woodfull famously remarked to 'Plum' Warner, the English team manager: 'There are two sides out there. One is playing cricket, the other is not. The game is too good to be spoilt.' It seems strange, I say to Tony, that Jardine had such a deep interest in Hindu philosophy. Jardine, insists Tony, was a monster. I know, I say, and yet he could be rather witty. Crusoe records how once, after an ultra-slow innings in a Test in Australia, Jardine apologised to an Australian for batting 'like an old spinster defending her honour'. That's not witty, says Tony, just sexist.

While Tony has been adding sexism to Jardine's other crimes, Daniel Vettori has taken guard, and left two balls from Powell to end the over. I enjoy watching Vettori bat almost as much as I enjoy watching him bowl his cunning spinners. He is a left-hander, wears glasses and has a rather unorthodox technique. His favourite shots are the cut and the pull, and he regularly manages to hit the ball to parts of the field other batsmen seem unable to reach. Still Lewis and no Edwards: Chanderpaul must be captaining on automatic. Or maybe Edwards really is carrying an injury and can be used only sparingly.

Lewis bowls another metronomic maiden to Astle. Powell continues to Vettori. This is Powell's seventh consecutive over since tea, quite a reasonable spell for a bowler of his pace, but the three wickets he's taken will have helped to keep the energy pumping. As if to contradict me, Chanderpaul's field placings for Vettori show thought. Vettori may only bat at number eight, but this belies his usefulness and nuisance value. He's made two Test 100s, and he scored absolutely crucial runs in the first Test. For him, Chanderpaul has set seven fielders on the off-side – two slips and two gullies, a point half-way to the boundary, an extra cover and a mid-off – and only two on the leg-side: a mid-on and a deep long-leg. The plan seems to be to feed Vettori's cut shot, to try to get him caught somewhere in that off-side ring.

Counter-intuitively, Powell bowls a half-volley, which Vettori drives back past him for four. Powell switches to round the wicket, and off the last ball of the over Vettori pulls a straight long-hop through the vacant leg-side to the boundary. Astle is sufficiently stirred by this to cut Lewis for another four.

258 for 6 off 70 overs, a lead of 66. Drinks with Astle on 30, and Vettori on 8.

Umpire signal: boundary four

We sit on the grass,

*sipping from plastic
water bottles,*

*discussing the best
of what we have
just done*

*and recalling
great matches.*

Tim Heath,
'Playing the game'

Drinks break

CRICKET IS A GAME rich in stories. One of my favourites concerns Geoff Boycott, the dourly selfish Yorkshire and English opening batsman. On the 1970–71 England tour of Australia, Boycott and Basil D'Oliveira were batting against Johnny Gleeson, whose 'mystery' spinners had been causing the side significant problems. Chatting between overs, D'Oliveira told Boycott he thought he had finally worked out Gleeson, to which Boycott, pointing to the players' dressing-room, apparently replied, 'Oh, I sorted that out a fortnight ago, but don't tell the other buggers up there.' This is so apt a story it ought to be true.

However, when my friend the historian and cricket writer David Kynaston and I recently went through the relevant *Wisden* trying to work out which match it might have been, we couldn't find one that fitted.

David tells an equally telling story about W. G. Grace in his book *WG's Birthday Party*. Over his long and phenomenally successful career, WG – or 'Doctor' or 'Doc', as he was also known – was as famous for his umpire-swaying as for his feats with bat and ball. In July 1898 his county, Gloucestershire, was playing Essex. The Essex side boasted Charles Kortright, arguably the fastest bowler there has ever been. In the first innings WG had made 126, and when Essex batted he took 7 wickets for 44 runs. David picks up the story in Gloucestershire's second innings:

> WG had made only six when he was caught and bowled by Walter Mead, but he refused to accept the umpire's decision and made him change it. The denouement came in a three-ball sequence the next morning: off the first, a thoroughly worked-up Kortright had WG transparently leg-before, but the umpire did not agree; the next WG snicked, but again the umpire turned the bowler down; the third uprooted WG's middle and leg stumps, making one of them do a complete somersault in the air. As WG stood unbelieving for a moment, his bat aloft, Kortright could not resist what would

become an immortal remark: 'Surely you're not going, Doctor. There's one stump still standing.'

Another favourite story, told me by someone who claimed to have played in the match, involves the great Pakistani all-rounder Imran Khan, when he was a teenager at school in Worcester. Already a pretty fast bowler, Imran used to sometimes turn out for the masters' team, usually just bowling off a couple of paces. On this occasion, the masters were playing a local village side.

Imran took a wicket. The incoming batsman had to pass him on his way to the crease. 'I'll get you, you black bastard,' he said. Imran said nothing, but measured out his full, very long run-up. The first ball caught the shoulder of the bat as the now terrified batsman desperately threw it up to protect his face – and went for six straight behind the wicket-keeper. The second ball hit the stumps at about the time the batsman was backing rapidly into the square-leg umpire. As the batsman passed Imran on his way back to the pavilion, Imran reportedly said, 'Well, at least you can say you hit Imran Khan for six.'

My own Imran Khan moment came at the Basin Reserve in the late 1980s, watching him captain Pakistan against New Zealand. It was an easy-paced pitch lacking bounce, what cricketers call 'a flat track'. New Zealand batting. A slow afternoon, match drifting, old ball. Imran idling at mid-off.

A wicket falls. Dipak Patel comes in. Imran knows Patel well from the English county circuit, where they have regularly played against each other. He promptly puts himself on to bowl. Instantly he is producing sharp reverse swing. Patel is out before the end of the over. Imran takes himself off. Point made.

Three more thrilling occasions as a cricket-watcher:

17 June 1966, the beginning of half-term break. A school friend has got the two of us tickets for the second day of England against the West Indies at Lord's. We arrive just after lunch to see England mop up the West Indies' tail (Ken Higgs 6 for 91). West Indies all out 269. This is almost unbelievable after their win by an innings in the first Test. But for me the real point of the expedition is that Graveney, at the ripe age of 39, is back in the England side after three years and 38 Tests in the wilderness. He is down to go in number 3.

Geoff Boycott and Colin Milburn open. Boycott in a cap: Mr Neat, as efficient as a saucepan. Milburn bareheaded, the Billy Bunter of batsmen, who always looks as though he's just raided the school tuck shop. All eye and forearms, he's a mis-hitter of the biggest sixes. But not that day: Hall has him lbw for 6. England 8 for 1.

Enter Graveney. Rounds of applause from the crowd. Wes Hall (fast), Charlie Griffith (fast and nasty), Gary Sobers (fast, slow, everything), Lance Gibbs (off-spin and cunning), David Holford (leg-spin): Graveney is facing the best attack in the world. He must be nervous, but it doesn't show. There is none of the playing and missing of five years earlier; his bat seems all middle. Soon he is leaning into the ball and stroking it through the covers. Boycott is admirably steady; Graveney makes it look easy. At stumps he is 65 not out. The next morning, like Fleming today, he narrowly fails to get his hundred. *Wisden* says he got out cutting Hall. That's not how I remember it. It was an attempted pull off the front foot, a favourite shot. I can still see him playing it on the TV screen.

14 February 1985, New Zealand v Pakistan, the final day of the third Test at Dunedin. New Zealand, 228 for 9, need exactly 50 to win. The last man, Ewan Chatfield, joins Jeremy Coney. I watch the *coup de grâce* on television. Martin Crowe has scored two immaculate 50s but it doesn't seem enough. The young Wasim Akram, in his first Test, has taken five wickets in each innings. He has already sconed the big-hitting Lance Cairns on the head, forcing him to retire. (Helmets are now regularly in use, but Cairns has unwisely eschewed them.)

Received wisdom says that Coney should score only singles towards the end of an over, and shield Chatfield from the strike. But the two soon drop this ploy, taking whatever runs they can and inching slowly and agonisingly towards their all but impossible target. Coney finally flicks a ball down to fine-leg, and they run the two required. It is, to borrow a phrase from the poet

Allen Curnow, 'something nobody counted on'. I haven't allowed myself to move a muscle for about an hour. When I try to stand up, my leg has gone entirely numb.

7 August 2005. I didn't watch this at the time, but thanks to a DVD given me by my youngest son, Tommy, I have now seen it several times. The English fast bowler Steve Harmison is bowling to the Australian number eleven, Michael Kasprowicz, at Edgbaston, in the second innings of the second Test against Australia. Australia are leading the series 1–0. Like Coney and Chatfield, the last pair, Brett Lee and Kasprowicz, have turned a certain loss into an almost victory. They need only three more runs to win as Harmison lumbers in, all arms and legs. He and Freddie Flintoff, both around Edwards' pace, have been trying yorkers, but the batsmen have been squeezing them away on the leg side.

Harmison bowls short, rising, into the body. Kasprowicz jerks back, throwing up bat and gloves in involuntary protection. The ball hits something – glove, bat handle, wrist, chest – and veers off down the leg-side. Geraint Jones, the wicket-keeper, dives a long way across and deftly catches the ball. Players, crowd, everyone, appeals. The flamboyant New Zealand umpire Billy Bowden raises his trademark crooked forefinger. Pandemonium. It is the defining moment of the series. England go on to win 2–1, regaining the Ashes for the first time in almost 20 years.

Umpire signal (Billy Bowden): out

For Daniel Vettori,
the sun

dips over a
shimmering pitch,

knocks out distant
island stumps,

spins on towards
the clouds.

Nicola Easthope,
'How does your sun?'

Evening session, continued

POWELL, AFTER HIS wicket-taking spell, is off and Gayle back on. Vettori immediately late-cuts him for four, a favourite shot. Lewis continues. As though to be fair to both spinners, Vettori late-cuts him too, also for four. Astle again seems not to be reading the googly, getting a couple of inside edges. But the total is ticking over, and another partnership seems to be under way.

Chanderpaul belatedly decides to mix things up. First, Bradshaw replaces Gayle at the R. A. Vance Stand end, then Gayle switches to the scoreboard end. Bradshaw continues to leak runs. But after only one over there, Gayle is off for Runako Morton, whom we haven't seen bowl before. Morton bowls at military medium pace, and Astle and Vettori easily milk him for seven. Astle brings up yet another Test 50 with a four flicked through square-leg.

Lewis returns. Astle and Vettori in turn milk him. That's 50 in 12 overs since drinks. Nothing extravagant, just sensible batting. The lead is stretching out with New Zealand now over 100 ahead.

This is not good bowling though. The West Indies teams of the 1970s to '90s would have slowed the game down. Clive Lloyd and Vivian Richards would have shuffled around their bevies of fast bowlers, set containing fields, really made the batsmen work for their runs. The same goes for the Australians. England won back the Ashes in 2005 because they were able to get good starts to most of their innings. McGrath was injured for two games, Gillespie and Kasprowicz under par − only Lee and the eternally mesmerising Warne kept the pressure on − and, even so, Lee and Warne alone were almost enough. The current Windies side lacks control, lacks talent. Not many Test sides would have let themselves be bowled out for under 200 by Franklin, Martin and Mills on this wicket.

Astle has played well, however, in his more circumspect vein, avoiding the lofted shots he loved in earlier days. His batting technique has never been exactly a model for youngsters. Like Andrew Jones in the

1990s, he tends to jump around too much, particularly against the short-pitched ball. But, like Jones, he has good hand–eye coordination, and rarely seems to be in trouble. Jones did often *look* to be in trouble, frequently playing shots with both feet off the ground, but the impression was misleading: he was a consistent scorer.

Astle has one shot that's especially distinctive as well as effective, a kind of scything pull across a raised left leg. It's not a way of playing the pull that you often see. As a child I had a cricket game in which one wheel determined the ball, and another a range of shots and sometimes dismissals. The picture for five runs – an unusual number in a real game unless there are overthrows – showed a batsman executing exactly Astle's scything pull shot.

Today, Astle has been scoring mostly with cuts and deflections. He takes another four to third man off Bradshaw. Bradshaw has gone for 90 off 18 overs, five an over. This is expensive for someone expected to do a stock bowler's job. Chanderpaul bowled him a lot in the first Test, overbowled him perhaps. Certainly he looks tired.

In 1957 at Nottingham, England went in against the West Indies with only four bowlers: Brian Statham, Freddie Trueman, Trevor Bailey and Jim Laker. They were lucky to bat first, and scored 619 for 6 declared (Graveney 258). Although Frank Worrell opened, and carried his bat for 191 not out, the West Indies were still made to follow on – that is, bat again – not having got close enough to the England first innings total. However, Bailey became injured, and an increasingly weary Statham, Trueman and Laker had to carry the load. Trueman had just been rested after a longish spell when a wicket fell, and the England captain Peter May called him back to bowl with the words, 'Come on, Fred, England expects.' To which Trueman is said to have replied, 'No wonder they call her the blooming mother country' – although 'blooming' is unlikely to have been the expletive used.

After another maiden from Lewis, Vettori cuts and glances Bradshaw for four and three to push the latter closer to his 'bowler's century' – 100 runs scored off a bowler in a single innings. Chanderpaul, whether from kindness or annoyance, takes Bradshaw off – and at long last brings back Edwards.

Edwards immediately goes around the wicket to Vettori, but in his first over his line isn't right, and he hasn't worked up to full pace. There's more effort in his second, a string of bouncers, two of which are called no ball. But they do the trick, because later in the over Vettori tries to pull another short one, is late on the stroke, and the ball lobs out to Chanderpaul at mid-on. Vettori leaves for 42, looking decidedly vexed. He and Astle have put on an excellent innings-righting stand of 86, but the dismissal was unnecessary. It's almost close of play, only an over and a half to go. He should have been there to resume tomorrow morning. A 50 was there for the asking.

This – a wicket late in the day – often happens, Tony and I remind ourselves from our elevated position. Sometimes a wee flurry, says Tony half hopefully. But not this day: Franklin and Astle see things through. Lewis doesn't quite achieve yet another maiden. He's never looked menacing but is the only bowler to have kept the runs down. His day's analysis of 26–8–57–0 is not at all a bad return. Astle has 65 and Franklin 2. New Zealand are 335 for 7 and lead by a healthy 143 with three wickets standing. The two batsmen and the West Indies leave the field, followed by the umpires. The crowd clap, begin to disperse.

Nearly 350 runs and 9 wickets. For the West Indies, Edwards has bowled fast and effectively, if too briefly, and Powell and Lewis have backed him up. Denesh Ramdin took that leaping catch. Chanderpaul mystified with his captaincy. For New Zealand, Fleming batted commandingly, with admirable support from Fulton, Astle and Vettori.

Tony and I pack up our things, push through the turnstile, and on the walk home begin again to analyse the day's play.

Death's sharp off-cutter has bowled him through the gate.

Harry Ricketts, 'Epitaph on an old cricketer'

Close of play

A FEW DAYS LATER I receive a call from Tony. A ten-wicket win's always a good win, he opens, though the Windies are pretty poor at the moment. But do you realise the thing we didn't have on Saturday? An lbw? I suggest, trying to remember if we had. Yes, true, no lbws, but also no run-outs, Tony says. Not a sniff of one. Unlike Brisbane, December 1960; he dangles place and date like a fly above the water.

You mean, I begin. Yes, that one, Tony cuts in. Benaud's Australians against Worrell's West Indies, first test of the series. Australia in the fourth innings need only seven to win with ten balls to go and four wickets left. What could go wrong?

But first Solomon runs out Davidson by a whisker. Next, in the very final over, Wes Hall has Benaud caught behind. Now it's five to win in seven balls, two new batsmen and only two wickets to fall. How many balls? I ask. Still eight-ball overs in Oz back then, Tony reminds me.

Then, of all things, Hall drops Grout off a dolly. Imagine the panic, the energy zipping round the ground. By now it's three to win in three balls. Meckiff heaves the ball towards the square-leg boundary. A four will do it. The batsmen, Grout and Meckiff, are running up and down. The crowd is going wild. The ball pulls up short. Hunte throws in to the wicket-keeper — all of 90 yards. Grout dives for the crease to complete the winning run, is run out. The scores are tied.

Kline comes in, Tony continues, the last man — as though I've missed the point. So it's just Kline and Meckiff now, and one run to win off two balls. Hall bowls. The ball goes out on the leg-side — near Solomon, again. The batsmen run. Solomon picks up and throws in one movement. He's square-on to the wicket, just has the one stump to aim at. He hits it. Meckiff is out — first tie in Test cricket. Three run-outs in the last two overs. Unbelievable. Now did I ever tell you the time I saw...

Umpire signal: out

A cricket fan's reading XI

Cricket fans, if desperate enough, will read almost anything about cricket. Here are XI of the dozens of books I've found myself returning to over and over again.

The Cricketer's Companion, Alan Ross, editor: Eyre Methuen, 1979
This anthology by Alan Ross, one-time cricket correspondent for *The Observer*, long-time editor of *London Magazine,* and poet, contains accounts of several famous matches, ancient and modern, real and fictional, as well as player profiles, and stacks of good poems. Personal favourites include Siegfried Sassoon's 'The Flower Show Match', A. G. Macdonell's 'The Cricket Match', Harold

Pinter's 'Hutton and the Past' and Ross's own poems. If, on some desert island, I were allowed only one cricket book, this would be it.

Beyond a Boundary, C.L.R. James: Stanley Paul, 1963
In a play on Rudyard Kipling's once famous line 'What do they know of England who only England know?' James starts with the proposition 'What do they know of cricket who only cricket know?' What follows is a strange and fascinating blend of history, ethics, aesthetics and politics, intercut with affectionate and knowledgeable profiles of West Indian greats such as Learie Constantine and George Headley.

Australian Test Journal: A Diary of the Test Matches Australia v England 1954–55, John Arlott: Phoenix Sports Books, 1955
Many consider Neville Cardus to be the doyen of cricket writers, but I prefer John Arlott's earthier style. Arlott produced several remarkable cricket diaries of tours and Test series, written day by day as the games unfolded. This one chronicles Len Hutton's last hurrah and the brief glory days of 'Typhoon' Tyson.

Crusoe on Cricket: The Cricket Writing of R.C. Robertson-Glasgow, Alan Ross, editor: Pavilion Library, 1985
Together with Neville Cardus, R.C. Robertson-Glasgow ('Crusoe') is often credited with turning cricket writing into an art form. This compilation includes his cricketing

autobiography *46 Not Out*, with its evocative picture of English cricket in the 1920s, and many of his vivid pen portraits of the great players of the 1920s and '30s.

The Cricket Match, Hugh De Selincourt: Jonathan Cape, 1924
The classic novel about village cricket.

A Tale of Two Tests, Richie Benaud: Hodder and Stoughton, 1962
Australian Richie Benaud provides one of the best insider views of Test cricket ever written. He captained Australia in both these matches: the 1960 tied Brisbane Test against Frank Worrell's West Indies and the 1961 Ashes-deciding Old Trafford Test against Peter May's England.

The Young Cricketer's Tutor, John Nyren: Davis-Poynter, 1974
Originally published in 1833, Nyren's book includes 'Full directions for playing the elegant and manly game of cricket', and 'The Cricketers of My Time', Nyren's reminiscences of the great Hambledon players of the 1770s and '80s. The 1974 edition has an introduction by John Arlott.

The Art of Captaincy, Mike Brearley: Hodder and Stoughton, 1985
Mike Brearley, England captain from 1977–81, is widely held to be the best cricket captain there's ever been. In this wise and humane book, he gives advice to would-be

captains and provides a gallery of real-life cricketing characters, anecdotes and vignettes.

WG's Birthday Party, David Kynaston: Chatto & Windus, 1990
The July 1898 Gentlemen v Players match at Lord's was selected to celebrate W. G. Grace on his fiftieth birthday. Kynaston's brilliant account of the game explores the characters of those involved (including Grace's inimitable own) and offers a sharp sketch of the late Victorian world.

Cricket's Great Entertainers, Henry Blofeld: Hodder and Stoughton, 2003
Veteran English cricket writer and commentator Henry Blofeld pays tribute to the players from all over the world who have most delighted the crowds since the days of Alfred Mynn in the 1830s. Besides Gilbert Jessop, Keith Miller, Gary Sobers, Barry Richards, Sachin Tendulkar, Imran Khan, Muttiah Muralitharan and many others, Blofeld also salutes fellow writers and broadcasters such as John Arlott and Alan Gibson.

Rain Men, Marcus Berkmann: Little, Brown, 1995
Most so-called funny books about cricket aren't. This one is. It describes the lamentable history of a team of cricket addicts and no-hopers.

IDEAL WORLD TEST XI

1   W. G. Grace (England, 1880–99)

2   Jack Hobbs (England, 1907–30)

3   Don Bradman, captain (Australia, 1928–48)

4   George Headley (West Indies, 1929–53)

5   Sachin Tendulkar (India, 1989–)

6   Gary Sobers (West Indies, 1953–73)

7   Adam Gilchrist, wicket-keeper (Australia, 1999–)

8   Shane Warne (Australia, 1991–)

9   Sydney Barnes (England, 1901–13)

10 Dennis Lillee (Australia, 1970–83)

11 Muttiah Muralitharan (Sri Lanka, 1992–)

IDEAL NEW ZEALAND TEST XI

1   Glenn Turner (1968–82)

2   Bert Sutcliffe (1946–65)

3   Stephen Fleming, captain (1993–)

4   Martin Crowe (1983–95)

5   Martin Donnelly (1937–49)

6   John Reid (1949–65)

7   Chris Cairns (1989–2004)

8   Richard Hadlee (1972–90)

9   Ian Smith, wicket-keeper (1980–91)

10   Daniel Vettori (1996–)

11   Jack Cowie (1937–49)

Umpire signal: wide

Select glossary

all-rounder Player good enough at batting and bowling to be chosen in either capacity. Great all-rounders include Keith Miller (Australia), Gary Sobers (West Indies), Ian Botham (England), Kapil Dev (India) and Imran Khan (Pakistan).

Ashes Trophy held by Australia or England, whichever is the current champion in their ongoing rivalry. The name derives from England's first defeat by Australia in England in 1882. In mock mourning at this cataclysmic event, an obituary appeared in the *Sporting Times*, 2 September 1882: 'In Affectionate Remembrance of ENGLISH CRICKET, which died at the Oval on 29th August, 1882. Deeply lamented by a large circle of Sorrowing Friends and Acquaintances, R.I.P. N.B. – The body will be cremated, and the Ashes taken to Australia.'

When an England team 'regained the Ashes' a year later, a group of English women gave the captain, the Hon Ivo Bligh, a small urn containing the ashes of a set of bails which they had burnt. On Bligh's death in 1927, the urn was bequeathed to the MCC.

average Batsman's average score over a series, a season or a career. In Test cricket, a career average in the 40s or above is the usual benchmark for a good or great player. Australian Don Bradman's Test average of 99.94 is more than 35 runs higher than that of any other serious contender.

back foot The foot nearest to the stumps as the batsman takes his stance at the crease — the right foot in the case of a right-hander. A back-foot shot (such as a square cut or hook) is one played by the batsman with most of the weight on the back foot, which has usually been moved closer to the stumps.

backlift The movement by which the bat is brought backwards and upwards before being swung forward as the batsman plays the stroke. Fast bowlers confronted with a batsman with a high backlift will often try to york him, particularly early on.

bails Short lengths of wood which sit in grooves on top of the three **stumps**.

ball tampering Illegal changing of the condition of the ball by the fielding side. Ball tampering, in some form or other, is probably as old as cricket itself. Fast bowlers sometimes 'pick' or lift the seam of the ball to create more bounce and lateral movement when the ball pitches. Bowlers or fielders who scuff up one side of the ball (perhaps with fingernails or a bottle top) hope, by changing the aerodynamics of the ball, to make it reverse swing in the air.

batting crease *see* **popping crease**.

beamer Full toss aimed at the batsman's head.

bodyline Form of persistent, short-pitched fast bowling aimed directly at the batsman's chest and head with the intent of hitting him, or inducing him to give a catch in self-defence. This unsporting tactic is always associated with Douglas Jardine, captain of the 1932–33 MCC tour of Australia, who used it as a way of trying to curb Donald Bradman's batting genius.

bosie *see* **googly**.

bouncer Short-pitched ball which usually reaches the batsman at shoulder height or higher; *also known as* bumper.

boundary Either the outer ring of the playing area, indicated by a white line, rope, fence or some agreed limit, or a ball hit by the batsman beyond this limit without bouncing (scoring 6) or after bouncing (scoring 4).

bowled Form of dismissal whereby, after being delivered, the ball breaks the batsman's wicket, dislodging one or more bails.

bowling crease White line alongside and to either side of the two wickets.

breakback Old term for a ball delivered by a fastish bowler which 'breaks back' at the stumps from the off-side. The 1890s English fast bowler Tom Richardson was noted for his breakback.

bump ball Ball hit by the batsman, which bounces before being caught but gives the illusion of being a catch.

bunny Derisory term used of a feeble batsman, usually a tail-ender; sometimes also used to describe a higher order batsman who is out frequently to the same bowler. *Also known as* rabbit. *See also* **hoodoos**.

caught Form of dismissal whereby, after being delivered, the ball strikes the batsman's bat or gloves and is caught by a fielder before hitting the ground.

cherry Term used for the cricket ball, because it's also red. Hence 'new cherry' for the new ball used at the start of each innings, and available again during an innings after 85 overs. In one-day cricket, a white ball is used.

chinaman Mirror image of a **leg-break** delivered by a left-arm bowler; a left-armer's **off-break** to a right-handed batsman. The name is said to derive from Ellis Achong, a West Indian of Chinese descent who bowled in this fashion. Famous bowlers of the chinaman include 'Chuck' Fleetwood-Smith (Australia) and Johnny Wardle (England).

cover Fielding position on the off-side between extra cover and point. These three positions are generally referred to as 'the covers'.

cover-drive Forcing shot on the front foot to the off-side of the bowler, passing through the cover area.

declaration When the captain of the batting side decides to close the **innings** before all ten wickets have fallen.

deep mid-wicket *see* **mid-wicket**.

deep square-leg *see* **square-leg**.

dolly Simple catch.

doosra Leg-break bowled with an off-break action; very rare.

duck When a batsman is out without scoring a run. To be out first ball is to achieve a golden duck.

extra cover Fielding position on the off-side between cover and mid-off.

flipper Ball bowled by a leg-break bowler which, instead of breaking, 'hurries' straight on and often results in an **lbw**.

front foot For a right-handed batsman, the left leg that is advanced to meet a pitched-up ball or **full toss**.

full toss Ball which arrives at the batsman without bouncing. *Also known as* full pitch.

French cut When the ball hits the inside edge of the bat and passes between the batsman and the wicket. *Also known as* Chinese cut or Harrow drive.

get off the mark When a batsman scores his first run.

golden duck *see* **duck**.

googly **Off-break** bowled with a **leg-break** action; invented by B. J. T. Bosanquet and in Australia still often called a 'bosie'. The greatest googly bowler ever was probably the 1930s Australian 'Tiger' O'Reilly, who bowled at a brisk medium pace.

gully Close catching fielding position on the off-side round from **slip**.

handled ball Form of dismissal whereby the batsman deliberately touches the ball while it is 'live' with the hand not holding the bat.

hat trick Feat of the same bowler taking three wickets with three consequent deliveries. The term derives from the nineteenth century custom of presenting the successful bowler with a new hat.

hit wicket Form of dismissal whereby the batsman breaks the wicket with his bat or any part of his person in the course of making a shot.

hoodoos Word derived from 'voodoo', meaning a magic spell, usually bestowed with evil intention. A bowler is said to have the hoodoos on a batsman when he frequently gets him out, and so is perceived to hold the moral advantage. Another way of saying this would be that a particular batsman has become a particular bowler's 'bunny'. It used to be said in the 1940s and '50s that

Australian opening batsman Arthur Morris was England opening bowler Alec Bedser's bunny. More recently, English opener Mike Atherton was often called Australian opening bowler Glenn McGrath's bunny.

hook Cross-batted shot played to a short rising ball and hitting it to the leg-side, usually behind rather than in front of square-leg.

howzat? Appeal made to the umpire by the bowler and/or the fielders to give the batsman out. *Also known as* how's that? how was he?

innings Either a batsman's personal turn to bat, or that of the side as a whole.

in-swinger Ball that swings in the air towards the batsman from off- to leg-side. *See also* **swing**.

late-cut Stroke played at last possible moment to a ball on the off-side, usually sending it through the **slip** region. Dorothy Sayers' detective Lord Peter Wimsey was said to have 'a highly characteristic late-cut'.

lbw *see* **leg before wicket**.

leg before wicket (lbw) Form of dismissal where the ball, after being bowled and without first touching the batsman's bat or gloves, strikes the batsman on some part of the body in front of the wicket and would, on appeal, have gone on to hit the wicket in the opinion of the umpire. This also applies to balls hitting the batsman outside the off-stump if he doesn't play a shot. It never applies under any circumstances to balls which first pitch outside the leg-stump. (See figure 2, page 9.)

leg-break Ball spinning from leg-side to off-side (see figure 4, page 71). Famous leg-break bowlers include Arthur Mailey (Australia), 'Tich' Freeman (England), Clarrie Grimmett

(Australia), B. S. Chandrasekhar (India), Abdul Qadir (Pakistan) and Shane Warne (Australia).

leg-cutter Delivery which behaves like a fast leg-break but is created by 'cutting' the fingers across the seam, rather than by twisting the wrist. Alec Bedser (England) was famous for his leg-cutter, with which he dismissed Donald Bradman on a few occasions.

leg glance Shot played off either front or back foot by turning the face of the bat at the moment of impact with the ball, the ball going down in the direction of fine- or long-leg. K. S. Ranjitsinjhi (England) perfected this shot in the 1890s.

leg-slip Slip, but on the leg-side.

long-hop Short-pitched ball which sits up, asking to be hit.

long-leg Fielding position on leg-side on or near the boundary and between square-leg and fine-leg.

long-off *see* **mid-off**.

long-on *see* **mid-on**.

long-stop Fielding position on the boundary directly behind the wicket-keeper, standard in the eighteenth century and still common in junior cricket.

maiden over Over during which no runs are scored off the bat.

mid-off Fielding position next to the bowler on the off-side. Long-off is a mid-off on or near the boundary.

mid-on Fielding position next to the bowler on the on-side or leg-side. Long-on is a mid-on on or near the boundary.

mid-wicket Fielding position on leg-side, midway between the two wickets not too far out. Deep mid-wicket is a mid-wicket on or near the boundary.

nightwatchman Lower order batsman sent in late in the day's play to shield a better batsman from the bowling.

no ball In general, the call made by the bowler's umpire if the bowler oversteps the **popping crease,** or by the square-leg umpire if he considers a particular delivery by the bowler is a **throw**.

off-break Slow ball spinning from off-side to leg-side (see figure 4, page 71). Famous off-spinners include Jim Laker (England), Hugh Tayfield (South Africa), Lance Gibbs (West Indies) and Muttiah Muralitharan (Sri Lanka).

off-drive Forcing shot on the front foot to off-side of the bowler.

on-drive Forcing shot on the front foot to on-side or leg-side of the bowler.

out-swinger Ball that, when bowled, swings in the air away from the batsman and to the off. *See also* **in-swinger** and **swing**. Great out-swing bowlers include Fred Tate (England), Ray Lindwall (Australia), Freddie Trueman (England) and Dennis Lillee (Australia).

pair Score a duck in each innings of a two-innings game.

pitch *see* **wicket**.

point Fielding position square of the wicket on the off-side. The name dates back to the eighteenth century and derives from the term 'point of the bat', when the fielder stood very close in to the batsman.

popping crease Marked white line, parallel to the bowling crease, at or within which the batsman usually stands when facing the bowler, and outside of which he can be run out or stumped (see figure 1, page 7). The bowler, when delivering the ball, must have some part of his foot behind the popping crease. *Also known as* batting crease.

pull Cross-batted shot played to a short ball, 'pulling' it to the leg-side. Similar to the **hook**, but usually played in front of **square-leg**.

retired hurt If a batsman is injured during the course of play, he may leave the field and return at a later stage during the same innings. English batsman Colin Cowdrey, after having his arm broken by a Wes Hall delivery at Lord's in 1963, famously returned to the crease at the fall of the ninth wicket with two balls of the match to go and England requiring six runs to win. He stood at the non-striker's end while David Allen played out the last two balls to secure a draw.

reverse sweep Attacking cross-batted stroke with reversed hands played to the off-side to a pitched-up ball (*see* **sweep**). This is one of those strokes which make the batsman look foolish if he gets out playing it.

reverse swing Ability of a bowler to make the ball swing in the opposite direction to the way the batsman expects, usually caused by one side of the ball becoming roughed up. Sometimes called 'making the ball go Irish'. *See also* **ball tampering.**

runner Member of the batting side allowed to run for an injured batsman (but not face the bowling).

run out Form of dismissal whereby the batsman has failed to reach (or regain) the crease while taking a run.

short-leg Very close catching position on the leg-side, usually square to the batsman; you can also have forward and backward short-leg. Why these are not also called silly, as in silly mid-off, is a mystery.

short mid-wicket Fairly close (but not silly) position on the leg-side, midway between the two wickets.

silly mid-off Very close catching position on the off-side in front of the batsman. Its name seems to derive from its foolhardiness.

silly mid-on Equivalent of silly mid-off on the leg- or on-side.

silly point Very close catching position on the off-side 'at the point of the bat'.

slip Close catching fielding position next to the wicket-keeper on the off-side, as in first slip, second slip and so on. The name derives from the eighteenth century, when a snicked ball was called a 'slip' from the bat. Great first-slip fielders include Wally Hammond (England) and Bobby Simpson (Australia). Great second-slip fielders include Jeremy Coney (New Zealand) and Ian Botham (England).

square-cut Shot played square on the off-side with a horizontal bat. The late eighteenth century batsman William Beldam ('Silver Billy') was renowned for his cut shot. John Nyren says of Beldam in *The Cricketers of My Time* that 'when he could cut them at the point of his bat, he was in all his glory'.

square-leg Fielding position on the leg-side, square of and roughly in line with the batman. Deep square-leg is a square-leg on or near the boundary.

stance Position batsman adopts, waiting for bowler to come in to bowl. Most batsman stand at the **popping** or **batting crease** with their feet fairly close together and parallel to the crease, bat handle held in both hands, bottom of the bat on the ground behind the back foot, and looking over their left shoulder (for a right-hander) at the bowler as he approaches.

stump Part of the **wicket**.

stumped Form of dismissal whereby the wicket-keeper, with ball in hand, breaks the wicket after the batsman has strayed outside his crease while playing or after playing the ball.

sweep Cross-batted stroke played to the leg-side to a pitched-up ball. The adventurous English batsman Denis Compton was famous for his sweep shot.

swing Inward or outward movement of ball in the air after it is bowled, usually created by a combination of overcast atmospheric conditions and shine preserved by the bowler on one side of the ball. The ball tends to swing most when new and shiny, but *see also* **reverse swing**.

take guard When, at the beginning of an innings, the batsman holds the bat upright on the batting crease, asks the umpire for 'one leg' (leg-stump), 'two legs' (middle-and-leg-stump) or 'middle' (middle-stump), and makes a mark at the appropriate spot on the crease. The term 'guard' comes from the notion that the batsman is 'guarding' his wicket.

third man Fielding position on the off-side behind the batsman's wicket, covering the **slip** and **gully** area and usually towards or on the boundary.

throw Illegal delivery of the ball with a jerking action; the subject of much recent debate in relation to bowlers such as Muttiah Muralitharan (Sri Lanka). Notorious throwers include Geoff Griffin (South Africa), Tony Lock (England) and Ian Meckiff (Australia).

twelfth man Substitute player allowed to field if someone is injured, or needs to leave the field for some other reason. A twelfth man is not allowed to bat.

umpire Adjudicator. One umpire stands behind the **wicket** at the bowler's end; the other stands square on the leg-side along the line of the **batting crease**. The main responsibilities of the bowler's umpire are to call 'over' after six legitimate balls have been bowled, and to adjudicate appeals for **lbws**, **catches** and

run outs at his end. The square-leg umpire principally decides **stumpings** and **run outs** at his end.

underarm The original way of delivering the ball until overarm bowling was legalised in 1864. There were underarm bowlers in first-class cricket until after the First World War. In a notorious incident in a one-day match in 1981, the Australian captain Greg Chappell ordered his brother Trevor to bowl the last ball of the match underarm along the ground to prevent the New Zealand number eleven batsman attempting to hit a six to tie the game. The incident has been immortalised in *The Underarm*, a New Zealand play by David Geary and Justin Gregory.

wicket Either the three stumps the batsman defends and the bowler tries to hit, or the stretch of ground (22 yards/20.12 metres long and 10 feet/3.04 metres wide) between the two stumps. *Also known as* the pitch.

yorker Straight ball which passes **full toss** beneath the batsman's bat.

SOURCES

The author and publisher gratefully acknowledge the following sources of poems and passages in this work:

A Dictionary of the English Language, Samuel Johnson, 1755

'When an Old Cricketer Leaves the Crease', Roy Harper: *HQ*, May 1975

The Cricketers of My Time, John Nyren, 1833

'Cricket' in *All Cretans Are Liars*, Anne French: Auckland University Press, 1987

'At Lord's' in *Collected Poems*, Francis Thompson: Hodder and Stoughton, 1913

'The Crickets' in *Favourite Monsters*, James Brown: Victoria University Press (VUP), 2002

Crusoe on Cricket: The Cricket Writing of R. C. Robertson-Glasgow, Alan Ross, editor: Pavilion Library, 1985

J. M. Barrie, quoted in *Autobiography*, Neville Cardus: Collins, 1948

Bomber Wells, quoted in *Runs in the Memory: County Cricket in the 1950s*, Stephen Chalke: Fairfield Books, 1997

John Arlott on Cricket: His Writing on the Game, David Rayvern Allen, editor: Willow Books, 1984

B. J. T. Bosanquet, quoted in *The Ashes*, Ray Illingworth and Kenneth Gregory: Collins, 1982

'Childish Recollections' in *Hours of Idleness*, Lord Byron, 1807

The Viewing Platform, Ian Wedde: Penguin, 2006

Martin Crowe: Tortured Genius, Joseph Romanos: Hodder Moa Beckett, 1995

'Quote … Unquote', Harold Pinter

Beyond a Boundary, C.L.R. James: Stanley Paul, 1963

'Cricket' in *Taking Off*, Brian Turner: VUP, 2001

'Playing the game', Tim Heath (unpublished)

WG's Birthday Party, David Kynaston, 1990

'How does your sun?', Nicola Easthope (unpublished)

'Epitaph on an old cricketer' in *Your Secret Life*, Harry Ricketts: HeadworX, 2005

ACKNOWLEDGEMENTS

I would like to thank David Kynaston, Jonathan Millmow and Hamish McDouall for suggestions, and Tony Schirato for coming to the day's play with me and being such good company. Thanks, too, to Martin Crowe, Executive Producer: Cricket, SKY Television, for providing a copy of the day's play of March 18, 2006 as an *aide memoire*.

H. R.

Umpire signal: bye